God's Gift

— *a witness to His mercy & grace*

by Lillian Joseph

The message of this book is written to the Glory of God. From Him we receive our many gifts; from Him we received the gift of our daughter.

All thanks and praise to God alone!

All Glory be to God
In His Service
Lillian Joseph

Apollo Books
107 Lafayette Street
Winona, MN 55987

My Thanks To You

Esther Stinnett for editing and typing the manuscript,
God Bless You!

Marion Glinsmann for designing the cover and for
her many words of encouragement.

Jack Remmel for his work on the pictures and for
his help and concern.

To all that gave permission to include articles, that
provided information included in the book,
or in any way gave me the courage to write
this book.

To Kathy's husband, Bill, for his consent and added
input.

Above all, to those that showed kindness and
concern to Kathryn, Bill, Bob, and me
during her illness, and through your
kindness have allowed your name to be used
in this book.

To God Be the Glory

ISBN 0-916829-10-3

Manufactured by Apollo Books, 107 Lafayette St., Winona, MN 55987

PRINTED IN THE UNITED STATES OF AMERICA

Λ

I

Although she was driving through an area blessed with rich natural beauty, the nurse was unaware of the surroundings on her way to work at the Billings hospital that morning. Almost daily travel along this route had made the trip so familiar that her body maneuvered the car safely along while her mind concentrated on the job ahead.

Preparing patients for surgery was an interesting job — there were new faces and new challenges every day. She could comfort and encourage patients with the anticipation of relieved pain, the expectation of restored health, or the hope of the freedom of greater mobility.

But that day was different. What do you say to a twenty-seven year old woman facing brain surgery? What kind of comfort do you offer to a patient for whom the doctors have little hope? What kind of encouragement do you give a patient who knows her surgery will leave her blind?

She was a good nurse. Her uniformed presence usually radiated confidence, a confidence born of knowledge and skill.

But that day she was different. Oh, she was still a good nurse, but briefly her confidence had yielded to a feeling of inadequacy. She had driven twenty miles and still had no answers to her questions. She entered the patient's room still wondering what she should say.

My day would be different too. I had awakened that morning to a feeling of fear. Our daughter was scheduled for surgery in a few hours. The doctor was planning to remove a brain tumor that had entwined itself around her optic nerve. I feared for Kathy's life; I shuddered when I thought of her physical condition should she live. We knew she would be blind, but we didn't know what other complications there might be. My fear had intensified throughout the morning. There I was in Kathy's room trying not to let my fears show, fighting to keep the tears from coming.

As the nurse entered the room, Kathy was reminding me of God's love for us. She chided me for being so near tears when I should be trusting God. She knew beyond a shadow of a doubt that whatever the outcome of the surgery would be, God would work it for our good. She continued to speak of her confidence in God as the nurse shaved Kathy's head in preparation for surgery. The shaving was nearly finished, and Kathy was resting quietly when suddenly the nurse stopped her work. She had been thinking about all that Kathy had said; she needed to talk with Kathy. She told us of the anxiety she had experienced driving to work that morning and explained her apprehension at entering the room. She considered it an important part of her job to prepare her patients mentally for surgery—to encourage them, to send them to the operating room with an optimistic attitude. But, instead Kathy had been the comforting one; she had encouraged the nurse with her cheerful voice and message. Kathy had taken advantage of another opportunity to share her love for God. Shaking her head, the nurse returned to her work, and Kathy resumed her witnessing.

Kathy's testimony had been no surprise to me; it was what I had learned to expect from her.

Feeling utterly helpless, I watched Kathy being taken to surgery. As they left the room, I heard the nurse, astonished at Kathy's calm and faith-filled acceptance, ask a new question: "What kind of girl are you?"

What kind of girl indeed! Her 5'1" frame may have given the impression that she was just a girl. How misleading. That small body housed a woman; a woman wise beyond her years—for she had looked at, argued with and come to accept her impending blindness and possible death. Kathy was a child in only one sense; and that she would always be—a child of God.

'What kind of girl are you?' The question sent my mind on a journey back through the years, through the years of experiences that had shaped our daughter into the remarkable lady she was that morning——

Bob and I had been thrilled to learn that we were to be parents. There was concern and disappointment over the Army's orders stationing Bob in Germany. He would be overseas when the baby was born. We filled our remaining time together with making plans and sharing hopes and dreams. My parents agreed with our plans. I would live with them; the baby would be born in Miles City, Montana. Bob's dream included a daughter; we would name her Kathryn Louise, a tribute to our maternal grandmothers.

Our plans and dreams became a reality when our beautiful baby girl was born on August 28, 1952. On September 14th, God reached down and claimed Kathy as His own through the Sacrament of Holy Baptism. The Holy Spirit planted in her heart on that day the gift of faith, a faith that He would strengthen in her throughout her short life span.

Kathy and I were at home on my parents' farm. My sister, sister-in-law, and three brothers vied with each other for the chance to give the baby attention. The bond that developed between Kathy and her grandparents in those seven months would be important in the coming years.

Bob returned from Germany in March, his military obligation completed. Though Kathy was seven months old when Bob came home, she was not afraid of him. She was instantly at home on his lap and in his arms. Another important bond for Kathy began forming.

Though not financially wealthy, we treasured an abundance of love in our little family. We established our home in Billings, Montana, a city in which Bob and I had previously lived. Bob returned to work for McKesson & Robbins Drug, an association that would last for thirty-six years. I resumed my career as a hairdresser.

Church activities formed a major part of our family's life. Kathy was taught to respect God's house and began attending Sunday School regularly when she was four years old. Daily devotions at home reinforced that education. Praying was a natural part of Kathy's life. Even as a child, she was able to express her feelings to God and turned to Him for answers to problems she didn't understand. As a toddler, she had chosen my red prayer book as a

3

constant companion. She carried it everywhere she went, even cutting new teeth on it. After starting Sunday School, she would hold the book solemnly, singing her made-up prayers to her friend Jesus.

It was just a five-hour drive from Billings to my parents' farm so we were able to visit each other occasionally. Kathy would stay on the farm with Grandma and Grandpa for a few weeks when Bob and I returned to Billings to work. She enjoyed "helping" Grandpa with his chores and having cousins nearby with whom to play.

Kathy was three years old the first time she rode the bus there without Bob or me. We took Kathy onto the bus and told her she was to stay right there until she saw Grandma. When the bus reached its destination, the driver had to ask my mother to get on the bus—Kathy wouldn't budge until she saw Grandma.

Bob's parents lived in Nebraska, and we would spend some vacation time with them each year. Kathy looked forward to the trip and to renewing her friendship with her cousins there. Her Nebraska family would be even more important to her in the years ahead.

My work as a hairdresser provided Kathy with the opportunity to be a model. Every year the hairdressers in Billings present a fashion show exhibiting the latest hair styles. Kathy would often model for me and was usually the only child model in the show. The hustle and bustle of rehearsal would fascinate Kathy, yet she would stay exactly where I told her to stand. One year Kathy's self-control impressed one of the adult models so much that she told Kathy she would bring a present to her the night of the show. Kathy could hardly wait. She wasn't sure the lady would remember. She was thrilled when the woman brought her a doll in a beautiful red and white dress. It matched the red dress Kathy was wearing, and she carried the doll in the fashion show. After the show, the doll was given a place of honor in Kathy's doll collection.

Kathy had been born the same year the Lutheran Layman's League first aired its television program "This Is The Life." That fact became important to her in 1957 when both became five years old. Kathy was chosen to appear on television with our Pastor to celebrate the fifth anniversary of the television program.

Kathy and I were ready to go. She loved dressing up for special occasions and was looking forward to being on TV. I was getting nervous. It was time to leave for the station and Bob wasn't home yet. I began to pace — where could he be? Kathy shook her little five-year old head at me, "Mommy, Daddy will be here. Daddy always makes it." She was right. Daddy did make it, and it was a wonderful day for Kathy.

Going Home

Holy Baptism

Burp Hard

Don't Cry

Daily Swim

Merry Christmas

Hello Dad

Sitting under the
Mulberry tree in
Nebraska

Grandpa & Grandma
Pretty Baby

Candid Camera

Pot & Pan War

A Fire!!

Showtime

Pretty Flowers

Rollie & Kathy

Here Piggy

What a Model

Fishy Fishy

II

Bob had attended Lutheran school as a child and realized that the Christian education received there had given him the foundation of his ever-growing faith. We were pleased that Kathy would have an opportunity to attend parochial school. She attended a private kindergarten as we looked forward to the opening of Trinity Lutheran School. She was a member of the first class of first graders at Trinity. The parochial school teachers had such a profound effect on Kathy's life that we could see her growing spiritually as clearly as we could see her physical growth.

Kathy was seven years old when she first experienced the reality of death. We had taken my parents with us on our vacation in early summer and then had spent the Fourth of July with them. On the 18th of that month, we received a phone call that my father had had a heart attack and died. His prior good health had left me totally unprepared for such shocking news; I needed some time alone with my grief. My bedroom provided refuge as I gave way to my tears. Remembering the understanding my dad had always given me, the times we talked and laughed, the traditional family holidays—remembering, and knowing it could never be the same again—I lay on my bed crying. I was oblivious to everything except my grief. The child's voice from the doorway penetrated my distress: "It's okay, Mama. Grandpa's in heaven with Jesus."

Kathy would miss Grandpa. Her days on the farm had been filled with life unlike that in the city. She had listened with Grandpa to the plaintive call of the cow separated from her calf, the too-deep-for-their-size quacks of the ducklings, the chirping conversation of the crickets. Grandpa had shown her the piglets with their fragile-looking pink skin; she'd laughed with him at the clumsy run of the graceless young calf. It was Grandpa who had handed Kathy the fluffy chick and watched as she gently stroked the downy head and sat enchanted by the peeping and cheeping of the flock. Grandpa had time. He always made time. He had shared those fascinating sights and sounds with Kathy; he'd opened her eyes to the wonder of God's creation. Suddenly he was gone. She understood. She knew that this death would change her life, but she could be happy for Grandpa. She understood that he had finally reached his goal, the goal of all believers—life forever with Jesus Christ.

Kathy's faith was growing and becoming a part of her everyday life. There were some lessons, however, she would have to learn the hard way.

By the time Kathy started school, we had built a new home which included my beauty shop in the basement. Part of Kathy's daily routine was a stop in the shop as soon as she got off the bus to tell me how her day had gone. It seemed strange one day she went directly to her room to change her clothes. I understood though when she called down to say it was such a nice day she wanted to ride her bike. I knew something was wrong when I heard her in the playroom just a few moments later. Looking in on her, I found her playing with a new set of toy dishes. When asked where she had gotten them, she hung her head and explained in a barely audible voice. We had given her $3.00 for school insurance, but it had only cost $1.50. She had taken the remainder to the shopping center after school and bought dishes.

The clerk in the store was a customer of mine. I called her to tell her that Kathy was on her way to the store to return her purchase. The clerk stood firmly as Kathy, tears streaming down her face, packed the dishes neatly in the box and apologized. This lesson in honesty stayed with Kathy throughout her life, and she would often mention it when anyone talked about dishonest children.

Although she was an only child, Kathy seemed able to surround herself with people. She had many good friends in school and loved to have cousins stay at our house. She was especially pleased when Grandma moved to Billings to live next door to our house. Kathy's first stop after school was Grandma's house. They would share

9

some milk and cookies and talk about Grandpa. They both missed him. Then Kathy would tell Grandma about her day at school and would not leave until Grandma had joined her in a good laugh at the latest school jokes.

Kathy was eight years old when she discovered her special talent; for the next twenty-one years, music would play a major role in her life. Her first piano teacher was Donna. Each week Donna would come to our home, teach the music lesson and then keep her hair appointment in my beauty shop.

Although Kathy loved music, she didn't always want to practice her lessons. Bob was the solution. Whenever he would sit at the piano with her, she would work and work to get her lesson right. Through the years, they would spend many happy hours at the piano, playing and singing together.

Their singing helped the miles fly by each summer as we drove to Nebraska to visit Bob's family and as we traveled to various parts of our country and Canada. Usually Kathy would fall asleep after a few hours of driving, but when she was awake, we would sing or play games. She loved to see which of us would be the first to see a deer. Try as she might, she seldom beat her dad. No matter who would win the contest, Kathy would laugh and be ready to try again. The deer had been seen; it was a victory for all of us.

As much as we enjoyed traveling and visiting with relatives, it was even more exciting when they would come to see us. A visit from Grandpa and Grandma Joseph for Christmas in 1960 was especially memorable. Because of Christmas vacation, Kathy was home all day to shower them with her hugs. Grandpa spent his time in the basement finishing our recreation room for us, while Grandma was upstairs sewing dresses for Kathy's dolls. Kathy was up and down the stairs, carrying cookies and coffee to Grandpa and checking on Grandma's progress with the sewing. Having lost one grandparent, Kathy realized how precious their love is, and she was quick to tell and to show them how much she loved them.

The house seemed quiet after Kathy's school vacation was over and the grandparents had returned to their home. The stillness would not last long.

Recognizing the importance of involvement in group activities, Bob and I supported Kathy's decision to become involved in

Brownies. She and her friend Vickie looked for a troop to join. The troop we found had an opening for an assistant leader. To enable the troop to continue, I accepted the position. Shortly after the first meeting, the leader moved from Billings and I was promoted.

The weekly meetings were moved to our basement. Fortunately my last customer on Brownie-meeting day was a school teacher who also appreciated the value of scouting. Before the girls arrived, I would prepare refreshments for them; then while they enjoyed their snack, I would do my customer's hair. While she was under the dryer, I would start the girls on their craft projects. They would continue to work on their projects, offering each other help and advice, while I returned to work. As I combed out the teacher's hair, the sounds of the girls' excited voices and laughter would drift into the beauty shop, and we would feel our spirits being lifted. It was worth every bit of inconvenience we had faced. After my customer had gone, I would rejoin the group for closing activities and send them on their way.

These happy times were to be recalled for me after Kathy's death when Bob and I received a letter from Kathy's friend Vickie. Under the letterhead "The Lord watch between me and thee, when we are absent one from another," Vickie wrote of the love and friendship she and Kathy had shared:

"....We were as close as sisters for many years. I still remember the good times we had together. She liked coming to my house because there were so many people (three sisters), a lot of activity, not to mention the confusion...on the other hand, I liked coming to your house because it was a mansion to me, she had a trundle bed, a playroom, a beauty shop — oh, the memories are so good, you both spoiled me when I stayed there.

Remember the play all of us kids put on for our parents in your basement?

And Brownies, Lillian, you were a great leader, that was so good for all of us little girls — plaster of paris, popsicle sticks, selling cookies — what fun!

And the fashion show Kathyrn and I got to be in, and dressing alike, all of the wonderful memories of long ago are still fresh in my mind.

11

We were best of friends for a long time. Trinity Lutheran School, operettas and choir were all such a treat. I am so thankful to God for blessing me with a religious upbringing. If it wasn't for what I learned throughout my early years at school and church and friends, I probably wouldn't be able to write this letter to you both. All it takes is faith in God."

The play; I had forgotten about the play. Vickie and Kathy often visited each other's homes, and our families became friends as well. One evening as Vickie, her sisters and parents were visiting in our home, the laughter of the girls playing in the basement punctuated our card game. We could hear them moving the basement furniture and wondered what they were doing, when the girls came up the stairs to invite us to an original theatrical production.

The little actors had set up a stage area, complete with curtain, and arranged the chairs for us to be the audience. The costumes consisted of clothing they found in the basement—Bob's old hat and some old dresses and shoes of mine. We laughed till we cried, cheering them on as they acted and sang their way through the play they'd written. We could see them echoing our actions. That evening we enjoyed their entertainment; there was time later to reflect on behaviors we would rather not have imitated. It was an enlightening evening.

As a student in the fourth grade, Kathy knew what her life's career would be. She had so much admiration for her school teachers, she knew she wanted to be one also. Her teacher had Kathy write to Concordia Teachers College in Seward, Nebraska. Her name was placed on their mailing list and she continued to receive the school paper until she became a student there many years later.

Kathy never wavered in that decision. Having made her choice, she worked resolutely toward her goal. Kathy took the instruction received in school very seriously, and tried to apply it to her life at home as well. This is evidenced by a letter she gave Bob and me as part of our Christmas present that year.

Aspiring to be a teacher did not prevent Kathy from attempting to play hooky. A mild flu was making its rounds at Trinity Lutheran School, and the students were returning to the classroom with marvelous reports of daytime television programming. We received a phone call from Kathy's teacher one noon telling us that Kathy was sick. Bob was home for lunch so he went to pick her up. On the way home, Kathy mentioned the television program she wanted to watch. Bob told her that being sick meant going to bed, staying in bed the rest of the day — and there would be no TV! Kathy didn't miss another day of school that year and had perfect attendance the following year.

We felt Kathy's dedication to school deserved recognition. The perfect reward presented itself when LaVerda, a friend of ours, informed us she would be taking her children to Nebraska for a visit. She and Bob had grown up in the same area; in fact, they had been schoolmates. She offered to take Kathy along on the trip. A trip to Grandma and Grandpa's — the perfect reward!

When Kathy returned, the words tripped over each other as she raced to tell us all the exciting news. She'd spent time at Bob's twin sister's playing with the cousins and Grandma, and Grandpa had taken her to see all the other cousins, and Grandma had the best cookies ever, and Grandpa let her help him mow the lawn (Wait — slow down and catch your breath!), and they went to church on Sunday where Dad went when he was a little boy and "Guess what!" They all knew me!" There was a break in the commentary just long enough for her to present us a napkin holder she had made for us, and she was off and running with news about all the relatives. For days, she would suddenly remember something she'd forgotten to tell us and would relive the excitement in her mind as she delivered a detailed description of each event.

Throughout her grade school years, those moments each day when Kathy would come down to my shop after having visited with Grandma continued to be very precious time. Each day she would share the special activities of the day with my customers and me. One day she mentioned her religion class, which prompted a customer of mine to ask Kathy about the Trinity. Kathy explained very clearly the doctrine of three distinct Persons in one divine Being; she distinguished the Father from the Son, the Son from the Holy Spirit, and the Holy Spirit from the Father, ascribing to each His work and attributes, at the same time stressing the unity in one divine being. As Kathy left, the customer commented on how well Kathy had been taught. I couldn't help but think of what a fine teacher Kathy would be.

Those special times were soon to end as explained in Kathy's autobiography prepared for a sixth-grade class.

My Life
By Kathryn Louise Joseph

It started August 28, 1952, at Holy Rosary Hospital 4:00 P.M. in the afternoon. This was in Miles City, Montana that a beautiful black-haired and blue-eyed baby girl was born. The parents, Mr. and Mrs. R. L. Joseph, named the cute little girl Kathryn Louise Joseph.

The next six months after I was born, my dad was away in the Army and hadn't seen me yet. It was sort of hard for my mother, but she made it. When my dad came home, he wasn't used to me crying or just plain used to me.

The years went by and I grew like mad. Although I don't know very much, but I know a little bit. When I was eighteen months old, a lot happened. Once I climbed a ten-foot ladder without my parents knowing it. At two or three a ladder almost fell on me. Then at five I started kindergarten. My birthday party picture was in the paper. When I was six and started school at Trinity Lutheran School, I had Vickie Vossler for a best friend. My first teacher was Miss Blessing, my second was Miss Beck, third Miss Duchow, fourth Miss Duchow, fifth Mr. Kreitzer, and sixth Miss Ninneman. I liked Miss Ninneman the best. In the sixth grade, we found out we were moving to Glasgow, Montana.

I'll be moving this Saturday, June 6, 1964.

14

My Promsie

(A gift to my parents, not only at
Chistmastime but all the year through.)
I promise to remember to thank God
for the good Father and Mother He
gave me, and to obey them. I will
help all I can and be happy to help.
  I will come when I'm called. I
will help wash dishs and help take
out the garbage. To do my home
work and to practice my organ. I
ask you, Mother and Father, to help
me to do all this by keeping this and
reminding me when I forget.

Kathryn

Ready for Kindergarden

I'm Six

I'm Ready

Kathy & Vicky

KOOK-TV Receives Citation

A citation for public service was presented to KOOK-TV, Billings, by five-year-old Kathy Joseph on the fifth anniversary of the TV series "This Is the Life." As old as the "world's most televised program." Kathy gave KOOK-TV a birthday cake. With Kathy are, left, Operations Manager Ed Peiss, and right, Pastor Paul M. Freiburger

Family Trio

I'm Seven

16

Kathy said good-bye to her friends at Trinity, to Grandma next door, to her music teacher, and many others to whom she'd become attached. Bob was looking forward to working as the Glasgow-area salesman for McKesson; I was busy with preparing for the move.

Everything went smoothly, and we were soon established in our new home. Any fears Kathy may have had about being lonesome were soon alleviated. She met Carolyn, our neighbor across the street and found out they would be attending the same church and Sunday School. Their friendship took root immediately.

Kathy continued taking piano lessons. We'd purchased an organ for our home, and Kathy felt honored to play for church. The Pastor would give her the hymn numbers for Sunday early in the week so she would have all week to practice for the service.

Attending public school was a drastic change for Kathy. She'd never heard the language some of the students used. Shocked by such behavior, she told us, "Boy, if only those kids went to Trinity. They'd get their mouths washed out with soap."

School was being conducted in shifts because of overcrowding. Kathy went to classes from 12:35 to 5:45. With time, she adjusted to the change and was able to maintain her high scholastic standards.

Kathy also enjoyed Bob's new position as a salesman. She would often wear samples of his merchandise to school and use some of his sample school supplies. When the students noticed something new and different, they would ask where she'd gotten it. She was happy to tell the students, "You can get it at the drug store. Just tell them Kathy Joseph has one." If the store hadn't bought the item when Bob had shown it to them, he would soon receive an additional order.

The fall of 1964 saw dramatic changes in Glasgow. The Air Base was closed, and by spring, many people had moved away. Carolyn's father was transferred to Washington, and once again, Kathy found herself saying goodbye to a dear friend.

The winter had been a particularly depressing one. Not only were we watching friends leave, the weather had been colder than usual, and winter seemed unwilling to come to an end. With the first hint that spring had arrived, a neighbor and I set out to get some plants and seeds for our yards. We had been to nearly every store when we thought of one more stop we could make. As we were

17

turning into the parking lot, our car was jammed from behind. Dazed by the blow, we both realized shortly that we were victims of whiplash.

Following the accident, I was plagued with severe headaches. I tried to return to work but was advised by my doctor to become a housewife.

The major portion of my time was spent lying down. Kathy's back rubs would provide some temporary relief, but I was still unable to do most of the housework. Kathy was very helpful throughout the house, especially in the kitchen. She was soon in charge of meal preparation as well as handling the cleaning responsibilities. She never complained about the extra chores or about the activities she missed because my illness required too much of our income.

The few hours I was up during the day would tire me, and I would be ready for bed early. Bob and Kathy shared an aversion to early bedtime. They had no difficulty in finding reasons to stay up late. Many evenings they would retreat to Bob's office, where he would do his paper work and she her homework as late into the night as they could. The rest was important for my health and their time together was important for Kathy's growing. Bob's temperament was the model for hers; they could find humor in almost every situation, and they would always be content with what they had.

Kathy had a knack for sewing and enjoyed the challenge of difficult patterns. She proved that at the young age of nine when she made her first dress. How proud we were of her when Peggy called, she had won first prize, a blue ribbon at the fair. Every student in the eighth-grade sewing class had to make a complete outfit. Their creations would then be modeled in a style show, and the best garment from each class selected. Kathy chose a lime green suit and even made a hat to match. Although she was proud of her work, she was certain hers would not be selected as the best garment. Her reasoning was quite simple, "Only the uppity-uppity kids ever win." As she stood in the winner's circle that night and received her carnation and round of applause, she knew she would be reminded of her prediction she'd made that evening. The victory was good for her self-confidence.

When we had moved from Billings at the end of Kathy's sixth grade, we had promised her that, if at all possible, she could attend the graduation of her classmates from Trinity School. Classes were completed in Glasgow on the third of June, and on the fourth, we put her on the plane to Billings. She was thrilled when her friends and former classmates had her join them for the class picture. So, although she didn't graduate with them, she was there in front and center in the picture that would enjoy a place of honor in her room. Those friends—Roger, Vickie, David, Rene, Leslie, and others—would continue to provide her strength for the test that was yet to come.

Kathy had confirmed her faith at Glasgow's Faith Lutheran Church. The verse selected for her was, "Be thou faithful unto death, and I will give thee a crown of life." Rev. 2:10b.

That spring my mother broke her hip in a fall. Unable to stay in her apartment alone, she spent time recuperating in her children's homes. Anxious to complete her convalescing at home, Grandma asked if Kathy could stay with her. Grandma was a very precise housekeeper and would sometimes forget how young Kathy was. Kathy was expected to scrub the floors as quickly and exactly as Grandma had before her accident. Grandma's neighbor Jeff came to Kathy's rescue, reminding Grandma of Kathy's inexperience and how helpful she was being. Grandma's appreciation grew as she got reacquainted with Kathy. She began to develop a patience she had never had and admired Kathy's ability to be content, even find humor, in every situation. Years later Kathy would be grateful to Grandma for the housekeeping lessons received that summer. They would often share a laugh over those days when they had learned from each other.

That August, after Kathy had returned home, Grandma and Grandpa Joseph came with Uncle Arnold and his family to visit. As always, we thoroughly enjoyed their visit; yet we couldn't help but notice that Grandpa's health was failing.

Kathy & Jan, 13 years old

Kathy's Room

Kathy at Recital

Homeroom Door

Prize
winning
outfits

20

Trinity Lutheran Billings
Vacation Bible School

12 Years

11 Years

8th Grade Graduation
Trinity Lutheran Billings

Amy's Sponsor

Confirmation-
Faith Lutheran

Kathy was baptized here;
now Neal's sponsor

III

Kathy met the challenge of high school studies with her usual enthusiam. She continued to study music and enjoyed learning to speak German. I had looked forward to sharing German with her, as that had been the primary language used in our home when I was growing up; however, I spoke a different dialect from the one Kathy learned, so the conversations in German were not to be.

Athletic events comprised a major part of the high school's social activities. Kathy was an avid Scottie fan, to the point of persuading Bob to paint her bedroom red and white. Her white canopy bed held a menagerie of stuffed animals, including the school mascot—a black Scottie wearing a red plaid coat.

Kathy was very actively involved in church work. She helped teach Sunday school, played the organ for worship and participated in the youth group. She took advantage of District-wide youth meetings to get together with her friends from Billings.

Kathy had thrived on the busy schedule of the school year, and knew she would need to find activities to keep her busy during the summer as well. That summer following her Freshman year she decided to look for a job. She was thrilled when she was hired by the A & W just one block from our house. She was told she was too young to be a carhop, but they would hire her to peel potatoes and onions and wash dishes. She was glad for that opportunity and jumped at the chance for the job. She kept that position until one of the carhops was sick; then Kathy was given a promotion.

That summer we traveled to Nebraska in June. Bob's Dad's health had continued to deteriorate; as we were preparing to leave, we found it more difficult than ever to say our good-byes. We wondered whether we would see Grandpa alive again.

As we returned for his funeral in August, we shared our memories of him. In our minds' eyes, we would always see him in bib overalls. We recalled the times he had spent with us; we told Kathy about his visit on her first birthday. We knew Grandpa was safe in the arms of His Savior. There was no sadness for him—he would no longer suffer the terrible headaches that had caused him agonizing pain—there was grief for the survivors. He would be missed.

We had a special surprise that September. Bob's brother Jerry and his family came to spend a weekend with us. We had a delightful day at Fort Peck Lake, a nice picnic spot with great fishing. I would, like to have stayed even longer, but as evening approached, Kathy and her Aunt Norma decided it was time to go home. Upon arriving at our house, we leisurely took turns getting cleaned up. As Bob and I, the last ones in the rotation, came out to the living room, we found it filled with friends and neighbors there to surprise us on our seventeenth wedding anniversary. Kathy had planned the whole party, made all the arrangements and paid for it with the money from her job. Her gift to us was a pair of wooden candlesticks. The greatest gift was her thoughtfulness and her concern for our happiness.

Highlights of Kathy's sophomore year were being selected to participate in the state music meet, singing in the state chorus, and a school mixed choral group. She also sang a solo at District Music Festival.

Kathy and her friend worked at mastering the art of throwing parties. They would decorate the basement with streamers, prepare snacks and set up the record player. Add a group of friends and their party was off and running. We always enjoyed having the kids at our house.

Following a summer that included driver's training, trips to Canada and the West Coast and deep-sea fishing, Kathy was ready to start her Junior year. Little Kathy in her little Volkswagon was a familiar sight around town as she continued her church work, music lessons, and school activities.

23

Homecoming was one of the first activities of the school year. Kathy worked hard on the plans and decorations for the special night. The team to beat was the Lewistown Eagles; and, surrounded by a cheering crowd, Glasgow did exactly that. Kathy was given the homeroom-door banner and was reminded of the big game every time she saw the banner on the bedroom door in our basement. School was off to a great start.

High school years are exciting. With the new maturity comes added responsibilities, privileges, and opportunities. Kathy thrived on each of these. Her friends and involvement in church and school activities became increasingly important. Consequently, Kathy was particularly frustrated when Bob told us in November that we would soon be leaving Glasgow.

Bob's job required a move to Lewistown. Once again our little family prepared to leave a home we'd grown to love, to say good-bye to friends we would miss, and to begin again with a new home, new friends, new church, and, for Kathy, a new school. The beginning anew was an exciting prospect; the leaving was an occasion for tears.

Our house sold shortly after Christmas, and, in the midst of a very cold winter, we made our plans to move. We were determined to have Kathy in Lewistown for the beginning of the second semester on January 20th. Kathy's friends gave a surprise farewell party for her. The group enjoyed an evening of bowling, followed by a slumber party at her friend Eileen's home. The gifts they gave her were expressions of their affection for Kathy and brought her enjoyment, especially in the early lonely days in Lewistown.

On January 19th we loaded our cars with everything we didn't want to freeze and with enough clothes to last Kathy for two weeks and headed for Lewistown. While Bob called on his customers, I emptied the carloads into a motel room and prepared a temporary home for Kathy.

Bob and I would need to return to Glasgow and complete the arrangements for the move to Lewistown. In two weeks we would rejoin Kathy in Lewistown, and we would move into our new mobile home.

It was hard to leave that night, but we knew the motel managers and their children would keep an eye on Kathy. Their daughter was just one year younger than Kathy and was to be a tremendous help to her. Kathy was less apprehensive about attending a new school since there would be one familiar face there. Kathy often shared a meal with their family also, and her days were less lonely because of the care they showed her. Driving back to Glasgow, we reminded ourselves that it would be just a few days before Bob would be back in Lewistown again. He called on his customers there on Monday mornings; with Kathy there, he would go down on Sundays and spend the day with her.

Winter was firmly entrenched; with the early dusk and delayed dawns of January, night seems to last forever. Although there was more than enough work to keep me busy, my thoughts were filled with concern for Kathy and even the fleeting daylight hours seemed to drag by.

We were told that as long as the temperature remained frozen near thirty degrees below zero, our mobile home could not be moved to Lewistown. Our home was sold; we had to move. Although Kathy was getting along fine, we were eager to be with her. The motel room became home to the three of us, ending our separation of two weeks. In the evening Bob would do his paper work on the table; Kathy her schoolwork at the desk; and I would try to stay out of the way.

After one month of this "togetherness", we were relieved to see the mobile home arrive, followed shortly by the moving van with our furniture.

Immediately Kathy and I started moving our possessions from the motel room. We didn't stop until everything was transferred, and we could spend that night in our new home.

Our lives began to resume a normal routine. We found a piano teacher for Kathy and, by Easter, she was helping out at church as a part-time organist. Our church in Lewistown was larger, and Kathy enjoyed the active youth group. She was making friends at school, but welcomed a weekend visit from her friend Eileen. The girls spent the weekend huddled in conversation. There was much to share.

Having been an "A" student at Glasgow, Kathy was assigned to an advanced math class. She struggled with the material, but just couldn't understand the lessons. After weeks of struggling, Kathy went back to Glasgow with Bob for a weekend and asked her former math teacher there for help. She was amazed that they'd put Kathy in such a difficult class. The weekend tutoring answered some of her questions, but math class continued to be more of a challenge than she wanted.

Report cards arrived and Kathy's fears were confirmed, Math—D. We phoned the teacher for a conference, but he insisted there was no need to meet. Kathy was a wonderful student, was improving, and would do just fine. With his assurance, Kathy relaxed and began to enjoy school more. She felt free to spend more time on music, even taking part in a musical. By the end of the year, she was at home in Lewistown and anticipating her Senior year. Even that final "C" in math did not dampen her spirits.

Kathy's plans to attend Concordia Teacher's College in Seward, Nebraska remained firm. Her enthusiasm increased after a two-week seminar at CTC following her Junior year. She was privileged to be chosen as a participant in the brief Fine Arts program that summer.

Adding to her summer excitement was the chance to visit with her relatives in Nebraska. Several of the cousins were near her age, and they shared tales of school experiences as well as dreams of the future. Although Kathy was usually separated from those relatives by a thousand miles or more, her special love for family kept them near her in her heart.

As usual, the summer went by all too quickly, and school and winter approached.

Kathy's loyalty was still divided; it was hard for her to break her attachment to the Scotties. Bob and I expected the football season to help her complete her transition, and we looked forward to the season. When the schedule was announced, we could hardly believe it. The opening game of the season would be in Lewistown, and the team to beat—Glasgow. What a blow! Kathy had given her Scottie homeroom-door banner to her friend Jerry before she left Glasgow, but the memories of that homecoming were still fresh in her mind.

The day for the big game arrived: September 7th, and it snowed all day. By game time, there was nearly a foot of snow on the ground. We were able to sit in the car and see the game. Our hearts ached for Kathy as we watched her standing at the side-line fence. She knew she couldn't cheer for Glasgow even though her heart was with them. She didn't cheer at all. Silently she watched her Scotties defeat her Eagles. Her loyalties divided, there could be no victory for Kathy that night.

Always anxious for new experiences, Kathy joined the speech team in her Senior year. She took part in speech meets in Lewistown, Malta and Billings. Each time Bob and I would wait anxiously for her return to hear how she'd done. Sometimes we heard the results on the radio before she arrived home. Her coach, Kurt Hodgkins, was excellent at encouraging the students and instilling confidence in them.

Kathy and her friend Marilyn would practice their speeches by presenting them to Bob. Finally he suggested they practice with a tape recorder so they could hear their own delivery. This rehearsal method helped each of them to improve their delivery techniques considerably, enabling both of them to compete in the State Speech Meet in Missoula. Kathy was eliminated in the semi-finals, but she had earned a trophy which she proudly displayed in her doll cabinet.

For Kathy the speech team was more than learning to speak in public and more than meets and trophies. Speech was people—a chance to meet new friends, an opportunity to care about more people. Kathy opened our home to the members of the team. We would never know how many of them would be staying at our house the night after an out-of-town meet.

The most challenging speech competition Kathy entered was the American Legion Democracy Contest. I didn't understand why Kathy was so nervous about this particular contest. After all, she had spoken before groups many times, and this time she was just speaking to the student body and the judges. Yet, as the day for the contest approached, her uneasiness was increasingly apparent.

The night before the competition, Kathy came to our room. Her reminder to us to come the next day had an urgent tone. I assured her I would be there. Her next request was even more urgent, "And will you pray for me?" Reassurance wasn't enough; Kathy needed to talk about this fear. Finally, she answered our questions. She was nervous because of speaking to the student body. The kids thought it was fun to heckle the student speakers. If a speaker should struggle for a word, the audience would applaud and further confuse the speaker. Kathy was so afraid they would distract her that she decided not to wear her glasses. Unable to see the students, she proceeded smoothly through her speech and won second prize.

A listing of Kathy's activities was included in the program book when she competed in the Central Montana Junior Miss Pageant:

Kathryn Louise Joseph
Fergus County High School

Kathryn is the shortest contestant in the pageant. She is 5'1-1/4" tall, has blond hair and blue eyes. She is the daughter of Mr. and Mrs. Robert Joseph. Kathryn sings and plays the piano. She is a member of the speech club. Kathryn participates in archery, bowling, swimming, tennis. She is a member of St. Paul Lutheran Church, Missouri Synod. She is assistant church organist, Sunday School teacher and a member of the choir. Kathryn will attend Concordia Teachers College to become a Lutheran elementary school teacher. She will do a vocal solo as her talent.

Kathy's solo was "My Favorite Things" from *The Sound of Music*. Receiving fourth place in the pageant was a bonus for Kathy, for she considered the experience itself worth all the effort she expended on her preparations.

Shortly after the pageant, Kathy took part in the school musical, *Plenty of Money*. She continued to give musical events and activities a favored position in her life. She was again selected to participate in the State Music Meet.

During her Senior year, Kathy was converted into a Fergus (Lewistown) fan. She was eager to attend the basketball tournament in Great Falls. Bob was involved in a sales meeting in Billings, so Kathy and I went to Great Falls with one of Kathy's girl friends and her mother. We had a great time at the tournament.

Just as we were beginning the 110-mile trip back to Lewistown, snow started falling. Visibility deteriorated; we were relieved to finally reach a truck stop. We were told there that the road conditions were better toward Lewistown than Great Falls. Slowly we made our way home, often traveling no more than ten miles per hour. Our prayers for protection became prayers of thanksgiving as we stepped into our home. The next morning, while Kathy was the organist for Sunday morning worship, our hearts were filled with praise for our loving God.

With the end of her Senior year approaching, Kathy wanted to look for a summer job. As her only work experience was that of a waitress or carhop, she decided to apply for work at the restaurants in Lewistown. I picked Kathy up after school, and we began the search for a job. Kathy had been told no at every place we had tried, when we stopped in front of the last restaurant on our list. Kathy asked me to pray as she went in to apply. She came out fifteen minutes later having been hired. She was scheduled to work the next evening, after school. Kathy made one request, that she not be required to work Sunday mornings. Her employer agreed.

In Glasgow, Kathy had often spoken of having a graduation party; we had promised her she could have the party of her choice. Then came the move to Lewistown and the party was never mentioned again, until—until just one month before graduation, when Kathy asked if she could still have her party. We were thrilled. Invitations were given to the entire senior class.

The day of graduation arrived. The seniors gathered for graduation rehearsal. As soon as their practice was completed, they came to our home. The pop company had set up tubs full of ice and assorted flavors of soda in the yard. We served 105 students and teachers a "Sloppy Joe" dinner. Kathy's Uncle Lawrence and Aunt Dorothy, Lori and Grandma helped serve the graduates. The students were a joy to entertain. They were polite and appreciative. Several years later three of these young men introduced themselves to me, thanked me again for the party and inquired about Kathy.

The graduation ceremony that night was the climax of a big day. Along with her diploma, Kathy was given the cash prize for placing second in the American Legion Democracy Contest. The boy sitting next to her whispered, "That's the fastest ten dollars you ever earned." He wouldn't have believed how hard she had worked to earn that money.

The students in the class had prepared their predictions of each one's future accomplishments. They prophesied that Kathy would become a missionary and work in a hospital. Her husband would have to be a minister.

Kathy had enclosed with her graduation announcement this notice: "I plan to attend Concordia Teachers College, Seward, Nebraska, to serve my Lord as a Lutheran School Teacher. I ask your blessing."

With college fast approaching, Kathy was fortunate to be able to change from part-time to full-time work at the cafe. Once again she had surrounded herself with people and soon became friends with the regular customers. One of her favorites was a 96-year-old man, Joe Montgomery, who came in every day and always wanted to be waited on by the young girl. Her wages and tips went directly into her college fund; daily she could see her dream coming closer to being reality.

When Kathy had applied for her job at the cafe, she had told them we were planning a vacation in June. Her boss was always very understanding and kind, and Kathy was given the time off.

On June 5th, we left for a two-week vacation to New York and Washington, D.C. We were determined not to waste a moment of our time and to see everything we possibly could. With Kathy going to college this fall, we knew this would probably be our last family vacation.

Our first evening in New York found us strolling in Times Square. Very quickly Kathy noticed that *Fiddler on the Roof* was playing, and we promptly purchased tickets for Sunday afternoon. A big day had already been planned for Saturday: visits to Hyde Park, Bear Mountain and West Point, and an evening of window shopping. Sunday evening Kathy's first-grade teacher and her husband came in from their home on Long Island and gave us a tour of Manhattan and Long Islands.

Monday featured an all-day tour of New York. Kathy continued noticing the plays, and we were thrilled to see *1776* that evening.

Bob had been a trusted employee of the same pharmaceutical firm for twenty-two years, so it was interesting to view their home office that Tuesday. A final tour Tuesday evening, Circle Line Tour around Manhattan Island, and we were ready to leave for Washington, D.C., the following morning.

Enroute to D.C., we were reminded of *1776* as we saw Independence Hall and the Liberty Bell in Philadelphia.

Thursday and Friday were filled with sightseeing in Washington, D.C., including a chance to observe—from Senator Mansfield's family gallery seats—the Senate in action. We were notified by McKesson-Robbins, Bob's employer, that they had made arrangements for us to see *Hello Dolly* that evening. Kathy was thrilled. After spending time visiting with friends in New York and Chicago, we arrived home relaxed and refreshed, ready for a busy summer.

Back at work, Kathy saved all the money she could. She had decided in grade school, at the same time she chose teaching as her future career, that she would pay for as much of her own college as possible. She had started her savings at that time, investing her money in the Church Extension Fund.

As we were driving to church on August ninth, we could see smoke rolling up from downtown area. Leaving the church services that morning, we learned that it was the Fergus Cafe that had burned. Kathy was concerned, not only about losing her job, but for her boss and how the loss of her business would change her life.

Just a few days later, with a good recommendation from her boss, Kathy was hired by another cafe. With the added business they received as a result of the fire, they needed more help.

Bob had another week of vacation coming, but he was not able to take it until September. Kathy had to be in Nebraska in August.

Bob's brother Reuben, his wife Evelyn, and their son Jerl came from Nebraska to visit us in August. They took Kathy back with them and helped her get settled in Seward. Their home in Hampton, Nebraska was just fifty miles from Seward. Kathy would spend a number of weekends with them during her college career and would soon call them her "parents away from home."

IV

We arrived on campus after Kathy had been in classes for ten days. She was lonesome for us but was busy making new friends and adjusting to college life. She had found a part-time job in the cafeteria so there was little free time in her schedule. In addition to her education classes, Kathy majored in music and minored in speech. She was glad Bob's family lived near Seward; she would be able to enjoy frequent visits with them.

Our visit went by quickly, and before we knew it, it was time to return to Montana. Having seen Kathy on campus, we knew she was as happy as she had dreamed she would be. In the few days she had been there, she had begun establishing new relationships and friendships as she found a new world of people to care about.

It was quiet at home with Kathy gone. We welcomed her occasional phone calls and read and reread the many letters she wrote. We treasured those letters; we knew she was very busy at school, and time was precious to her.

Kathy was honored to be chosen as a member of Concordia Singers, a select musical group which has opportunities to travel around the country. As she had become more familiar with the college, she'd found a job she enjoyed more and left the job in the cafeteria for one in the music library. It required many hours each week but she enjoyed every moment of it.

I was concerned as Thanksgiving approached. I knew the first holiday with Kathy gone would be a sad time for me, so I was glad we could celebrate Thanksgiving in Billings with members of my family. We knew Kathy would be fine. She would be in Hampton, with her Nebraska family.

Worshipping in Zion, Bob's church home as he was growing up, would help her feel close to us. Zion was a country church, and little had changed since Bob had worshipped there as a child. The ornately carved altar remained; the pulpit, also beautifully decorated, was a little balcony above the altar. Kathy felt at home, a member of the family.

Kathy would be sure to spend some time with Grandma on each visit. As she would leave, Grandma would send along some rolls or cookies for Kathy to share with her friends at Seward. Grandma loved to braid rugs, and Kathy would take any clothes she could no longer use to Grandma to be made into rugs. Grandma gave rugs to each of her grandchildren. Kathy enjoyed hers in her dorm room and saved one special one for her hope chest.

The busy days rolled by quickly for Kathy, and the end of her first semester neared. We were anxious for Christmas vacation and made arrangements for Kathy's airplane tickets. She wrote:

Say, I think those plane reservations are great. Just think, in three and one half hours and I'm home. That is great.

Well, one more week and my reading course is over. I have learned many skills to improve my reading and my study habits too. Now as I practice them in my studying, I see a little improvement all of the time.

We the American Guild of Organists club are going to Lincoln Monday for some function so I'll write you more about that later.

I'll close for now, and I'll write again, tomorrow or Saturday.

Be good, don't work too hard, and trust in God, and boy, everything looks brighter.

Love, Kathy

Kathy ended every letter with a reminder of God's love.

With her first semester of college behind her, Kathy flew into Billings on December 18. We enjoyed a visit with Grandma and attended the wedding of Leslie Rene, one of Kathy's school friends, before going home to Lewistown. There was time after Christmas for Kathy to work at the cafe, which had reopened in a new location. This gave her a chance to see many of her friends over her Christmas vacation.

Returning to Seward in January, Kathy quickly got back into her college routine. The Concordia Singers were preparing for their Spring Tour. For ten days they traveled to St. Louis, Indianapolis, Cleveland, Detroit, Milwaukee, and Chicago presenting as many concerts as time would allow. Kathy had often heard Bob say he would like to see the "Indy 500". On her return to Seward, Kathy called to say she had ridden around the race track in their tour bus.

Over the Easter vacation, Kathy was one of the group of students representing Ambassadors for Christ in Billings. They were in that area for ten days, witnessing in churches and going door-to-door conducting religious surveys. Five of the students, including Kathy, came to Lewistown for Good Friday. They made a radio announcement inviting people to church services that night. With the five young people staying there, our home seemed alive again.

By the middle of May, Kathy's first year of college was over, and she was home for two weeks. She was privileged to go on a European tour with a group from the college. They traveled throughout seven countries on the month-long trip.

While in Germany, Kathy met one of my cousins who lives there. She and Lilo had made arrangements to meet at the train station. Neither of them knew the other and were fortunate to meet; they had a nice visit. Kathy had also tried to arrange a visit with her cousin Larry who was stationed in Worms at that time. They were not so fortunate and missed each other at the station.

Kathy was the youngest member of the tour; she was thankful she had an opportunity to travel with fine Christian friends. She was especially thankful for Dorothy who loaned her money when she had spent all of hers. Kathy never told us she'd run out of money until she had repaid the debt.

The group arrived back in the USA on July 8th, just in time to enroll in the second session of Summer School. Kathy had decided to continue to attend college through the summers. In that way, she could complete college in three years. She had determined that she would not have been able to earn enough money in three summers to have paid for the fourth year of college. More importantly, she was eager to get started teaching. There was usually an urgency in her life to do things immediately.

The summer had begun with Kathy home for two weeks and ended the same way. Kathy spent her brief break between summer and fall terms relaxing at home. We arranged our vacation to take Kathy back to CTC by the end of August. We stayed for a few days getting Kathy settled in and then visited Bob's family.

In her second year at college, Kathy lived off-campus with fourteen other girls. They had their share of fun and even seemed to enjoy the added responsibilities. Kathy especially enjoyed the added independence.

The Concordia Singers often traveled to neighboring congregations to take part in church services. Occasionally we heard them on the radio, singing on the Lutheran Hour, a weekly broadcast.

The Fall Tour that year included visits to Dodge City, Kansas; Guyman, Oklahoma; Colorado Springs, and Denver, Colorado. We doubted that a tour would ever bring them closer to Lewistown, so we made arrangements to fly to Pueblo, Colorado. We enjoyed a visit with Bob's brother who lives there, and with them, attended the concert in Colorado Springs. The following day we traveled to Denver with the Singers, spending every moment possible with Kathy and attended the concert there also. Seeing Kathy in November helped the semester seem to go faster for us.

Kathy returned to Lewistown for Christmas. That year she had an extra three weeks at home, during which time she worked at Highland Park School for college credit. That experience convinced her even more that teaching was the career for her. She loved working with the students and returned to Seward for the second semester with added determination.

Music continued to play a major role in Kathy's life. The Concordia Singers visited Minnesota and North and South Dakota on the Spring Tour.

Kathy's time at home became shorter with each vacation. In order to finish in three years, she needed to attend nearly every class session CTC offered. Her last year there, she was the student advisor for ten girls in one of the campus houses. That meant she had to return to school a week early for training.

We had often talked about a trip to Europe but always decided we should save the money in case Kathy needed it for college. When Kathy was hired as a student advisor, she was certain she would not need more money and started encouraging us to take the trip. Two of my dad's sisters and several of my cousins lived in Germany. It was exciting for me to meet the family I'd often listened to my father talk about. He had come to the USA when he was sixteen and had never seen his family again.

Bob had written Kathy to tell her that someone would be traveling a very long distance to visit her. Upon returning to this country from our European vacation, we flew to Lincoln, Nebraska. Reuben and Evelyn met us at the airport and drove us to Seward to visit Kathy. We took advantage of the opportunity to listen to the Concordia Singers rehearse. It was great to see Kathy's house and meet the girls she lived with. Her letters were even more interesting when we had met the girls she named in her correspondence.

December came and Christmas vacation flew by. Once again Kathy had to return to college early. She was to leave for her student teaching assignment in January and needed to complete a three-week interim course before she could go.

On January 23rd, she flew to East Detroit to do her student teaching at St. Peter's Lutheran School. The congregation couldn't have been nicer to her. Her landlady showed her around Detroit and treated Kathy like a member of the family.

Bob had promised Kathy a car for graduation, and Detroit seemed like the perfect place to buy it. Her landlady's son-in-law, Mr. Sherman, took Kathy shopping, and they checked every brand to find just the right car for Kathy. At last they agreed; Kathy's new car would be a Sahara Beige Duster. She phoned her dad, informing him of her decision. Bob spent a few days looking at cars and reading about each kind. In the end he agreed; she'd chosen wisely. He made the necessary arrangements, and the car was hers. The day after she picked up her car, Kathy wrote us the following letter.

3-13-73

Dear Mom and Dad,

I have so many things I want to tell you in this letter that I hope I don't forget any of them.

First , let me tell you about my new Duster. I got it last night but not without scolding the salesman. He had shown the price of $2,468 (total without subtracting $50 deposit) to his boss for okay. He had forgotten to add on carpeting and price for bigger black sidewall tires. Anyway, he talked the boss into not charging me for the tires ($11.50), but he would have to charge me ($15) for the carpet. I didn't say any mean or nasty things, I just said that next time he had a customer buying a car, he should okay the price with the boss before he told the customer a final price. The total price of the car now is $2,485. I will send the sheet telling what everything cost.

I'm sending home all car receipts, etc., and would you put them in the bank safety deposit box for me?

I got gas in the car last night and even put nine whole miles on it (Ha!). It drives really nice. I know I will really be able to handle it easily....

I got a nursery rhyme book and an ABC book for Amy and Neal, respectively. I think they will like them and learn something from them. I got the books at our book fair. They are well constructed and have beautiful pictures....

Guess what happened to me at 1:30 A.M. this morning. I got a telephone call from someone. Guess who? Bob. I really couldn't believe it, but he had gotten the number here through information. He was quite embarrassed when I told him how late it was here so he didn't talk too long...

I miss having you here to talk to personally about this. I know God is working His will though.

It has been a pretty good week so far. Faculty meeting last night was really fun. It was at our principal's house. All of the teachers came and congratulated me on my new car purchase which made me feel good.

I'd better close and get ready for school. Please keep these car papers in an income tax file thing for me so I don't lose anything.

Love, Kathy

Soon it was time to return to college. Two of Kathy's classmates were doing their student teaching in the same area and rode back to Seward with Kathy in her new car. I knew just when they were leaving and the route they would follow. In my mind, I traveled with them across Michigan, Indiana, Illinois, Iowa, and finally into Nebraska. I imagined every conceivable problem along the way. Kathy called as soon as she reached Seward; she could hear the relief in my voice. "Mom," she gently chided me, "you know you didn't have to worry. We had Jesus with us, and He was watching over us all the way."

School activities took on a touch of sadness for some of the students as they began, one by one, to signal the end of college days. Kathy's final Concordia Singers tour would take her to Laramie, Wyoming; Provo, Utah; Reno, Nevada; San Francisco, San Luis Obispo, Downey, Orange, and San Diego, California; Phoenix, Arizona; Albuquerque and Santa Fe, New Mexico; Alamosa, Colorado and Ellinwood, Kansas.

As soon as we heard the itinerary, we notified friends and relatives in California that Kathy would be in their area. Bob's cousin Clara and her husband Carl drove from their home in Lake San Marcas to Orange. Kathy's hosts in Orange were related to friends of ours in Lewistown. Kathy had a great time seeing friends and relatives.

Kathy phoned us from Phoenix on the day before Easter. We were snowed in and laughed with Kathy as we compared the Arizona winter to Montana's.

The concert in Ellinwood brought out mixed emotions in Kathy. She loved singing; she especially loved to sing God's praises with her fellow Concordia Singers. She knew this would be the last concert of her last tour. While feeling sad that this, too, was coming to an end, she could rejoice in the opportunity to witness to one more congregation.

As graduation grew nearer, the students' thoughts became more occupied with wondering where they would be teaching. A Service of Presentation and Consecration was the first formal event in the placement proceedings. This was a very serious and moving service for the future teachers. Kathy sent us a bulletin so we could share in the message.

A SERVICE OF PRESENTATION AND CONSECRATION

Concordia Teachers College, Seward, Nebraska
Laetare Sunday, April 1, 1973, 6:00 P.M.
at St. John Lutheran Church

THE ORDER OF THE HOLY COMMUNION: (The Lutheran Hymnal, page 15 ff.)

THE PRELUDE

THE HYMN OF INVOCATION OF THE HOLY GHOST: WS 753

THE INTROIT: The Choir (The propers for Laetare are found on pages 63 and 64.) The Gloria in Excelsis is omitted during Lent.

THE EPISTLE: Galatians 4:21-31

THE GRADUAL: The Choir

THE GOSPEL: John 6:1-15

THE SERMON HYMN: LH 347 Cong. 1, 3, 4, 6. Choir 2, 5.

THE SERMON: "FOOLS FOR CHRIST"

THE OFFERTORY: "Create in me...."

THE ACT OF PRESENTATION AND CONSECRATION OF THE CLASS OF 1973 FOR THE TEACHING MINISTRY IN THE CHURCH

Director of Placement: Will the members of the Class of 1973 please rise? You have come together at this place and time to present and consecrate yourselves to ministry before God, the church, and this congregation. Therefore, I ask you now to affirm your intention to serve God and His people whenever and wherever you may be called to minister.

Class of 1973: We desire to serve God and His people as ministers of reconciliation, peace, and life. We ask God to use us in His Church according to His will.

Director of Placement: Please pray for me as I work in the days ahead to discover the opportunities for ministry in the Church so that you may realize your intention of ministry.

Class of 1973: O Lord, most gracious and loving Father, we ask You to bless the work of our brother, Professor Krause, in the days ahead as he strives to serve You and Your people and us. According to Your will, O Father, make it possible for us to serve as ministers of the life that Your Son, Jesus Christ, provides for all that believe. Bless the entire Board of Assignments and us, O Father, for the sake of Your Son, Jesus Christ, our Lord. Amen.

Director of Placement: Mr. President, the Class of 1973 is pleased to present itself—collectively and individually—to the Church. This class awaits the Church's call to service in places and among people where ministry can and ought to occur.

40

The President: On behalf of the Church, I accept with joy the Class of 1973 as another great gift that God gives His Church. Moreover, I commit myself to the task of working to place the members of this class so that they can use their abilities in the service of God and His Church. I now ask you, the Class of 1973, to consecrate yourselves to the God of all mercy.

Class of 1973: O Lord, most gracious and loving Father, we consecrate and dedicate ourselves to You as we await Your call to serve in the ministry of the Church. Strengthen and support us as we wait for that call and the opportunities it will present for ministry. Help us recognize also, O Lord, that we are already Your ministers, and guide us always so that You are served wherever we are. Bless Your Church and us, O Father, for the sake of Your Son, Jesus Christ, our Lord. Amen.

The President: The Lord needs your ministry. Go in peace!

THE DEDICATION OF ALL TO CONTINUING SERVICE

College President: The Lord of the Church calls upon each of us who bears the name of His Son to be "co-workers with Him." Each of us is already placed in that service, wherever we are, whatever our function is: whether we are students preparing for a special ministry, whether we are teachers or administrators right now; whether we are part of a supporting staff, or whatever our vocation is right now. Together let us acknowledge this and rededicate ourselves to an immediate and continuing ministry among one another by saying:

Congregation: All that we have, all that we are, O Lord, comes from You. Along with life and salvation You give us purpose in living. Help us day by day to see that purpose and to carry it out. As you have pledged Yourself to us through Your Son, our Savior, so we also dedicate ourselves

41

to Your service in Your world. Forgive our failings and strengthen us with word and sacrament to be a blessing to many. Send us forth in Jesus' name. Amen.

College President: Go forth in His name, supported with His power!

THE OFFERING

THE EUCHARIST

THE DISTRIBUTION

THE POST COMMUNION

THE POSTLUDE

The wait had begun. Not only did the students eagerly anticipate their placement, but parents, in homes scattered across the country, waited anxiously to hear where their son or daughter would be living in the coming year.

Nearly twenty days later the phone call finally came. Kathy's excitement could be felt in the sound of her voice. "Mom, I have a call. I have a call. I'm going to teach at Good Thunder, Minnesota. I'll teach third, fourth and fifth grades."

"Where is Good Thunder?"

"It's about fourteen miles from Mankato. South of the Twin Cities. Isn't it great, Mom?"

"Oh yes, Kathy, it's great! How much will they be paying you?"

"Oh, Mom," she chuckled, "that doesn't make any difference. The Good Lord will provide. I have a chance to teach; that's all I wanted."

Kathy sent the following announcement to our friends and relatives.

Greetings in Christ:

What a joy it is for me to send all of you this letter. On May 26, 1973 at 2:00 p.m. I will graduate at Concordia Teachers

42

College, Seward, Nebraska 68434—receiving my Bachelor's Degree in Elementary Education.

On August 15, 1973, I will report to St. John Lutheran School in Good Thunder, Minnesota, about 14 miles south of Mankato. I will be the 3-4-5th grade teacher. My call includes being church organist and choir director at St. John Lutheran Church, as well as my duties in my classroom. I am very excited about this and I am looking forward to my chosen profession.

The Bible passage I have chosen is one that all of us share. We, as Christ's disciples, are to spread the Gospel message to all, that they may come to faith in Christ through the Holy Spirit. I am very thankful that God has given me a special opportunity to teach His Word to children.

Also, I want to thank all of you, especially my Mother and Father and teachers, for making all of this possible for me. I hope you will help me share my joy and remember me in your prayers. If you are in the area of my school next year, do stop in and see me.

God's Blessings to ALL, Kathy Joseph

The Bible passage printed next to her graduation picture on the card she enclosed was, "Go then, to all people everywhere and make them My disciples: baptize them in the name of the Father, and of the Son, and of the Holy Ghost." Matthew 28:19

Bob and I arrived in Nebraska one week before the May 26th graduation ceremonies so we could visit with relatives and take part in the graduation week activities.

The first event on our arrival was a gathering we hosted at Reuben and Evelyn's home in honor of Kathy. Evelyn had made all the preparations for us. Many relatives and friends came to express their congratulations and good wishes to Kathy. She had time to visit with everyone.

Kathy's final concert with Concordia Singers also took place during that week. Their voices filled the air with their praise for God and the magnificent love He'd shown each of them.

The girls from Kathy's dorm planned a party to celebrate the coming of graduation and invited Bob and me to join them. We appreciated the honor of being included and happily accepted the invitation. They had chosen the local pizza parlor for the location. The sparkle in their eyes accented the laughter which carried on throughout the meal. Some of the girls would be back for one more year of college; some of them would be embarking on their teaching careers in the fall. All of them avoided any sad thoughts of farewell that evening. It was a night for fun and everyone had a great time.

It took two days to get Kathy's belongings packed. We sorted as we packed, loading separately in Kathy's car those things she would want to take to Good Thunder for the next year. Finally everything was packed and ready to go, just in time for graduation.

Both of Kathy's grandmothers, all of Bob's family from Nebraska, and Kathy's baptismal sponsor Aunt Phyllis were with us to witness this special day in Kathy's life. Just three years before I'd watched proudly as Kathy had received her high school diploma; I'd thought then of our little girl going off to college. Watching her receive that college diploma, I knew she was no longer a girl. She was a woman, trained and prepared to teach children, ready to embark on a lifetime of service to her Savior.

When the ceremony was completed, we took pictures, said our good-byes and began the long journey home. Bob and Phyllis drove to Baker, Montana and he went on to Lewistown from there. My mother, Kathy and I drove to Carroll, Iowa. We spent the night there with my brother Franklin and his family, driving on from there to Good Thunder.

What would the town be like? How large would Kathy's classroom be? These and dozens of other questions filled our minds as we neared our destination. We had planned to arrive in time for Sunday worship, but the weather didn't cooperate. Rain slowed our travel and we arrived as the service was ending.

Spotting our Montana license plates, people came eagerly to meet the new teacher. Kathy knew she'd found her new home. The people were friendly and more than willing to help. We were given a tour of the school, met the pastor and some of the school board members, and were introduced to Evie who offered to have Kathy live with her. They began visiting and found they immediately felt comfortable with each other.

We unloaded the items from Kathy's car, then had lunch with the pastor and his family. Good Thunder did not have a motel, so we drove on to Mankato. The next day we drove to Baker, spent the evening with my family, and returned to Lewistown the following day.

On June 10th we hosted a Graduation Tea for Kathy in our home. Bob and I were very proud of Kathy: She had completed college in three years, had her education completely paid for, and had been named to the Dean's list. She was a hard worker. The members of our congregation were pleased to have one of their young people going into full-time church work. Friends from church and from the community came to wish Kathy happiness and God's blessings. Having my mother and Cousin Doris from Billings there made the day complete.

Kathy was always happiest when she was busy. She had been in Lewistown but a short time when the cafe called and asked her to work for them. She welcomed the opportunity to earn some money; there were several things she wanted to buy for the coming year. She also looked forward to seeing all the people in the cafe.

Bob, Kathy and I flew to New Orleans that July where Bob was a delegate to the Synodical Convention of The Lutheran Church-Missouri Synod. It was an exciting experience for the family. Several students from CTC were serving as pages for the convention, and others, like Kathy, had come with their parents. Amid the hundreds of unfamiliar faces, it was refreshing to find some friends. While Bob's time was occupied with convention proceedings, Kathy and I were free to come and go. We rode the trolley cars and visited the ice cream shops. One evening we joined several friends for dinner in a Japanese restaurant. Sitting on the floor looked uncomfortable to me, so I was pleased to find there was a hole in the floor under the table through which we could dangle our feet.

We had just returned from vacation when it was time to prepare for Kathy's moving to Minnesota. On August 9th we hosted a farewell dinner for Kathy. We were pleased to have as special guests the Marquardts from Chicago. He had been principal of Trinity Lutheran School when Kathy first attended parochial school.

The following day we loaded Kathy's car and a rental trailer. Bob's job would keep him in Montana while Kathy and I would drive to Good Thunder. As soon as we were in the car, before turning on the ignition, Kathy said a prayer for our safe journey. God granted us a safe and a pleasant trip. Along the way we stopped to visit with Kathy's third grade teacher. She was pleased that her former student was following in her footsteps.

The teachers had to attend a workshop in Rochester on August 12-14. I stayed in Good Thunder to get Kathy's belongings unpacked and enjoyed getting acquainted with her landlady.

On August 19th Kathy and the principal were installed. The new principal had been a classmate of Kathy's at CTC and he and his wife had invited Kathy to their home for dinner on several occasions. A potluck dinner was served after the church service. It was an opportunity for everyone to meet the new principal and teacher.

That afternoon Kathy and I drove to Iowa to attend the wedding of a good friend from our Glasgow days. Ed and his friends had often visited our home; his service in Viet Nam had made that situation a reality for Kathy. After the wedding we had a short visit with my brother Franklin and his family. Then it was time for me to go home and for Kathy to begin teaching.

Kathy &
Bev, her
accompanist

High School
Graduation

Junior Miss

Ready for the Senior
Prom

German Hat

Family Picture

21 Years Old

College Graduation
Uncle Reuben & Aunt
Evelyn

47

New Car. Graduation.

St Peter school & church
East Detroit

Good Thunder St John's
Church & School.

Above: St Peters
Classroom. Right: Trinity
Lutheran School,
Fairbault Classroom

College Classmates;
Kathy's Student Advisers

Vacation

College
Graduation
Picture

48

V

Though Kathy was kept busy with all her responsibilities, she loved every minute of this new life. Yet she was ready for a break by November and flew to Nebraska to spend Thanksgiving as she had the past three years. It was a relaxing time for her, and she returned to Good Thunder ready to begin preparations for Christmas.

Back in Montana, Bob and I were counting the days until Christmas. We had made arrangements to fly to Minnesota to see Kathy's students' Christmas service and spend the holidays with Kathy.

We were met at the Minneapolis airport by Kathy and her landlady. We stayed at Evie's on Christmas Eve, following the Children's Service. On Christmas Day, after services, we drove to my brother's home in Iowa. The following day we went on to Nebraska to spend part of our Christmas vacation with Bob's family. It was the first time Bob had been in Nebraska at Christmas time since 1948 and the first time for Kathy and me.

Shortly after the first of the year Kathy found an apartment. It had been important to Kathy to have all her time free for teaching when she first started, but by January she was ready to add housekeeping responsibilities to her schedule.

Music continued to play a major role in her life. She bought a piano for her apartment and often talked about choir practice when she phoned. Soon, however, we noticed that she talked less about choir and more about a certain choir member. Bill became a major topic in our conversations.

Kathy's involvement in congregational activities increased as the year went on, so we were very surprised when she called to ask our opinion about a move. She had been offered a teaching position in Faribault, Minnesota. Teaching contracts are signed each spring; her decision had to be made quickly. After much prayer she was certain God wanted her in Faribault, and she accepted the new contract.

As soon as Kathy had completed her first year of teaching, she enrolled in a two-week college course at Mankato State College. Bill finished his college at that time.

Kathy had found an apartment in Faribault and I had offered to help her move. I took the train to Minneapolis and the bus to Mankato. Kathy was in class when I arrived, so Bill came to meet me. While she attended class, I packed her belongings in preparation for the move. The choir had a farewell party for Kathy, after which we said good-bye to Evie and drove to Faribault. Having unloaded everything into her new apartment, Kathy said her prayer for safety and we drove to Montana.

Summer was sailing along. Kathy worked at the cafe; we took a short trip to Calgary, Alberta, Canada; and letters from Bill arrived regularly. Kathy was eager to get back to Minnesota. Bill would be teaching in Winthrop, not far from Faribault.

Kathy never did say what was in that last letter from Bill, just that "it" was over. I was glad she had the job in the cafe; her boss was very understanding and for those hours each day her mind was occupied. During her hours at home, her eyes had a sad, far-away look that was very unusual for Kathy. She had always been content in whatever situation she had found herself.

The company Bob worked for often awarded household items as bonuses to their salesmen. Bob gave several of his prizes to Kathy to make her new apartment more comfortable and more attractive. That August they were loaded in the car with the rest of Kathy's things; she prayed, and we were off for Faribault. Once again she had teachers' workshops to attend, a new congregation to meet, a new home to get settled, and a new classroom to organize. I returned home on the train knowing Kathy would be busy. I hoped she would see Bill again; I missed the sparkle in her eyes.

Kathy enjoyed her new school. Serving as assistant organist instead of full-time, she had more time to prepare for her classroom. The lighter schedule agreed with her.

Bob and I had promised our nieces and nephews as they were growing up that we would, if possible, attend each one's wedding. The weddings that fall were a challenge. Our nephew Jan was married to Ann on September 23, and our niece Eileen married Dave on October 4. Kathy had been given time off to attend the weddings.

A few days before the first wedding, Bob and I drove to Minnesota; we had a few things to take to Kathy. We attended worship services in Faribault on Sunday; Kathy was the organist that morning. As soon as the worship concluded we began our drive to Nebraska. Kathy was pleased that being in Nebraska at that time would enable her to be with her Uncle Reuben and Aunt Evelyn on their 25th Wedding Anniversary.

Shortly after the wedding Kathy took the bus back to Minnesota. Jan and Ann had told us they would be traveling to Montana for their honeymoon, so we had given them a key to our home. On our return to Lewistown, we found they had already arrived and made themselves at home. What an honor it was to have them visit with us.

We just had time for Bob to complete a week's work while I cleaned everything from one trip and packed the bags for our return to Nebraska for Eileen's wedding. Kathy traveled to Omaha by bus, where she joined her cousin Jim for the drive to Hampton.

The day after the wedding Bob and I drove Kathy back to Minnesota. Bob still had a few days of vacation time and we wanted to spend them in Faribault. As we were traveling near Wintrhop, Kathy mentioned that Bill was teaching there. We could hear a catch in her voice and knew she was still lonesome. The weddings had been hard for her. She was happy for Jan and Ann and for Dave and Eileen, but the weddings had reminded her of her aloneness. Kathy had never had a lot of boyfriends, but had often stated that her husband must, above all, be a Christian; she also wanted him to have a sense of humor and to enjoy a variety of activities. She knew the Lord had someone for her. I hoped He would send that someone soon.

51

Bob and I were pleased to be able to visit Kathy's classroom one day. Bob went outside with the students for recess. As the children came back into the classroom the boys could hardly wait to tell Miss Joseph the big news; her dad was rich, he found 45¢ on the playground. They were even more excited when Bob put the entire amount in the class offering. Forty-five cents was a great deal of money to them.

The following morning we said good-bye to Kathy when she left for school, as we would begin our trip to Lewistown around noon. We bought a plant for her home and left it with our note to her. As we left her apartment, Bob commented on how happy she was with her home and her school. In my thoughts, I added, "If only that someone special would come..."

We spent that night in Bismark, North Dakota. After dinner we tried to call Kathy; her phone was busy. We continued trying for an hour, when her phone finally rang. The joy in her voice leaped from the phone as she told us she had just been talking with Bill. They would be going out for dinner Friday night.

Bill had been thinking of Kathy, too. After having mentioned her several times to the staff at his school, they began suggesting that he bring her over for them to meet. Their separation had only made each of them appreciate the other even more.

We continued our journey home, stopping in Baker to attend a wedding shower for our nephew Roland and his bride Beryl. They'd been married on September 27th.

We anticipated and enjoyed frequent calls from Kathy and treasured the joy we heard in her voice each time. The conversations centered more and more on activities she and Bill shared.

We were thrilled that Kathy was able to spend Christmas with us that year. At Faribault, the students presented their service early, so the teachers were able to spend the holidays with their families. Bill had given Kathy a very special necklace and a jewelry box, which she treasured. The vacation went quickly, but we knew Kathy was ready to return to Minnesota; she missed Bill.

In February Bob received word that his sales territory was being changed. Malta and the towns east of there were being assigned to a different sales representative, while Great Falls was being added to Bob's area. The company had decided that we would not have to move; the territory could be worked from Lewistown, but Bob would have to travel—a hundred and ten miles before he could call on his first customer on Monday morning. We had sold our house and were renting, so a move would not have been too inconvenient, but we were happy we didn't have to leave all our friends.

We continued to hear about Bill from Kathy. He had given her a pot of six tulips for Valentines Day. She was thrilled with the unusual gift. She was ecstatic when she called to say they were engaged. The Lord had indeed sent her someone special.

Although they'd talked on the phone, Bob and Bill had not met. Bob had heard so much about Bill he felt he knew him; but having a week of vacation coming, Bob eagerly made plans for an April trip to Minnesota to meet his future son-in-law.

A week was hardly enough time to travel to and from Minnesota, to meet Bill and his family and make some wedding plans. We made every minute count, all the while enjoying the visit. Bill and Kathy were eager to show us the house they'd chosen to live in after their marriage. We were glad we had time to see it. It would be a lovely home for them.

I had taken along some samples of wedding invitations so they could choose the style they wanted. The order would be placed as soon as the date was set. They also selected their napkins and we agreed the rest of the plans could be made over the phone.

Kathy arrived in Lewistown in the middle of June. The wedding would be August 3, so her summer would be busy. The first order of business was getting the invitations in the mail. The maid of honor and bridesmaids' dresses had been ordered, but Kathy wanted to make the dresses for the flower girls.

We were unable to find the material Kathy wanted for the flower girls' dresses in Lewistown, so we decided to go to Billings and combine a shopping trip with a visit to Grandma. As we were approaching Billings after a brief shower of rain, we reached the top of the hill, looking down into the valley and saw the most beautiful rainbow we had ever seen. We were both so struck by its beauty that we stopped the car for a chance to just sit and look. We couldn't help but remember God's promise and feel His love for us.

Kathy had decided she wanted to wear my wedding dress. Very little alteration was required for the dress to be beautiful on her. It was hard to imagine that twenty-five years earlier I had worn the very same dress on my wedding day.

There were several things to be moved to Minnesota since Bill and Kathy had gotten their new home. Once again we loaded Kathy's car and a trailer and drove to Minnesota. Kathy had moved her belongings from Faribault after school was out, and Bill was already living in the home. The new furniture had arrived and the home looked very comfortable. We unloaded the furniture and decorator items we'd brought; I was pleased that so many of the items we could no longer use would once again be put to use.

Another cousin of Kathy's was getting married in Nebraska that June. Bob was unable to attend, so Kathy and I combined the trip to Minnesota with one to Nebraska. Cousin Jim and Kathy were married on June 28 in Omaha. Bill went along with us and met all the Joseph relatives. They would be in Lewistown for Bill and Kathy's wedding in August, but Bill knew he would have more time for visiting at someone else's wedding and welcomed this opportunity to meet Kathy's family.

Following Jim and Kathy's wedding, Bill accompanied us to Montana. There were more relatives to meet. Kathy's aunts had planned a shower for her, to be held in the church at Plevna. They invited Bill to the shower also. Some of the relatives at the shower would not be able to attend the wedding in August and they took advantage of the opportunity to meet Bill.

Upon our arrival in Lewistown, we learned that Bob had received a call from his employer telling him that they thought it would be better if he lived in Great Falls. Bob knew they were right, yet the wedding plans had gone too far to change the location at that late date.

Bob and I went to Great Falls to find a home for us to move into after the wedding. While we were busy with house-hunting, Bill and Kathy transposed music for the brass quintet that would play at the wedding, met with the pastor for counseling and with the organist for rehearsal.

The women at the church gave a shower for Kathy and Bill. It was especially nice to have Bill included in the wedding showers. The love that was shown to them made us realize how much the members of a church family mean to each other.

Bill and Kathy found it necessary to make a quick trip back to Minnesota. At that time the Lutheran Women's Missionary League was holding its international convention in St. Paul, Minnesota. Kathy and Bill encouraged me to ride back with them. They would take me to the convention, complete their business and pick me up again. It was a very enjoyable trip. The two days of convention were inspiring and I had time to get better acquainted with Bill. On the way back to Montana he practiced his solo for the wedding. By the time we reached Lewistown he knew it perfectly.

The final week before the wedding was filled with last minute details. We had motel rooms reserved for all the out-of-town guests. Most of them arrived on Saturday, had lunch at our house, and checked into their motel. The wedding party met at the church that afternoon for rehearsal, followed by a buffet dinner for the wedding party and relatives. Bob's mother and oldest brother were unable to attend, but the rest of our brothers and sisters and my mother were there. Bill was the first in his family to be married and all of his family was there.

The following account of the wedding appeared in the Lewistown newspaper:

St. Paul Lutheran Church in Lewistown was the setting for the Aug. 3 afternoon wedding uniting Kathryn Louise Joseph and William F. Zastrow.

Candelabras with white, pink and burgundy ribbons flowing with springerli fern and bouquets of pink roses decorated the altar.

The double ring ceremony was performed by Rev. Robert Bohlmann of Lewistown and Rev. Herbert Schiefelbein of Good Thunder, Minnesota.

The bride is the daughter of Mr. and Mrs. Robert Joseph of Lewistown. The groom's parents are Mr. and Mrs. Raymond Zastrow of Good Thunder, Minnesota.

The service opened with the processional and the lighting of the candles by Waynbe Sackschewsky and Gene Joseph, cousins of the bride. Wedding banners, made by the bride and groom and honoring the Holy Trinity, were carried by Brian Pinnow, Scott Pinnow and Max Spiker, cousins of the bride.

"*Jesu, Joy of Man's Desiring*" was sung by the groom, accompanied by the organist, Grace Pennock.

A brass quintet comprised of Rodger Bacon, Ward Rikala and John Gordon of Lewistown and Craig Pinnow and Kim Pinnow of Baker, cousins of the bride, accompanied by the organ, sounded the introduction to "*Praise to the Lord, the Almighty, the King of Creation.*" The bride entered, escorted by her father, and the congregation sang the hymn with the accompaniment of the organ and quintet.

The bride sang "*Entreat Me Not to Leave Thee*" immediately following the marriage vows and she and the bridegroom joined in a duet, "*Let Us Ever Walk with Jesus,*" after the marriage candle ceremony.

The bride wore her mother's wedding gown of ivory slipper satin, featuring a victorian neckline, a low bertha collar above the deep basque bodice. Her long, lilly-pointed sleeves added to the period of styling. The full skirt flowed to a cathedral train and was bussled for convenience during the reception. The sunburst lace head piece was designed from her mother's veil and was fashioned to hold a full cathedral ivory nylon English illusion veil splashed with appliqued lace. She wore traditional blusher. A broach worn by her paternal grandmother was her only jewelry.

The bride carried a white Bible, topped with a white orchid, surrounded by white stephanotis and pink elfe.

Lois Sackschewsky, maid of honor, and Wanda Maier, bridesmaid, both cousins of the bride, wore gowns of shocking pink triple knit with sheer bishop sleeves. The neckline and cuffs were accented in 3-D veniese lace. Their pink garden hats were etched with deep burgundy velvet ribbon to match their escorts' jackets. They carried white fans with a corsage of pink phileanopsis orchids, accented with burgundy ribbons.

The flower girls, Julie Bohlmann and Amy Joseph, were gowned in pink flocked, flowered organza over taffeta, made by the bride. Their headpieces matched the baskets.

Neal Pinnow was the ring bearer. He wore a burgundy jacket with black pants. The bride is godmother of Amy Joseph and Neal Pinnow.

Denis Schiefelbein of Good Thunder attended the groom as best man. Charles Sundeen, Winthrop, Minn., was groomsman. Both are friends of the groom. They wore coordinated burgundy tuxedos with pink shirts.

Steven Pinnow, a cousin of the bride who is serving with the United States Marine Corps at Camp Pendleton, Calif., and Carl Zastrow of Good Thunder, brother of the groom, seated the guests.

For her daughter's wedding, Mrs. Joseph chose a mauve hand-brushed printed gown of imported chiffon styled with a Grecian crossed bodice and flowing back panel. Mrs. Zastrow wore an ivory interlock knitdress featuring a print of clusters of green and gold flowers accented with burnt orange. Both mothers wore white orchids.

An honored guest at the wedding was the bride's maternal grandmother, Mrs. Fred Pinnow of Billings.

A reception around the pool at the Yogo Inn was hosted by Mr. and Mrs. Reuben Joseph of Hampton, Nebr., aunt and uncle of the bride. The refreshment table was attended by the sisters of the groom, Mary Ann Zastrow of Rochester, Minn., Karen Zastrow of Wells, Minn., and Lynette Zastrow of Morton, Minn.

Mrs. David Brhel of Denton, Nebr. was in charge of the guest book. Anita Joseph of Hampton, Nebr., and Brenda Sackschewsky assisted with the service folders. Barbara Joseph and Debra Joseph from Hampton, Nebr., cousins of the bride, assisted with the gifts.

A wedding dinner was served in the Yogo Inn Sapphire room to all the guests, with the uncles and aunts of the bride and groom acting as table hosts and hostesses.

Mrs. Robert Bohlmann baked and decorated the large cake that graced the table. Its tiered columns gave the effect of a church sanctuary with a miniature bride and groom and their attendants on a spiral staircase. Small cakes in the shape of a cross were baked and decorated by the mother of the bride.

Jake Roberts provided organ music for the wedding dance that followed the dinner.

Following a trip to Winthrop, Minn., where they will live, the couple spent their honeymoon touring places in the surrounding area.

The bride will teach the nursery school at Gaylord Lutheran School in Gaylord, Minn., this fall. She will also be choir director at Redeemer Lutheran Church in New Ulm, Minn. The groom is a librarian at Winthrop High School.

As each guest arrived at the wedding, they were handed a little scroll with the following words along with the bulletin:

This is the day we vowed our love
Before our friends and God above.

In years to come as we recall,
Again we'll thank you, one an all.

All of you who come from far and near,
We're grateful for your presence here.

And may God bless you, this we pray,
As He has us this wedding day.

Kathy and Bill
August 3, 1975

Our 25th Wedding Anniversary wasn't until September 3, however, the relatives would not be able to return at that time, so we celebrated that evening also. Bill and Kathy made their way to the honeymoon suite as the rest of us danced the night away.

The next day the relatives came to our home, said their good-byes and family after family started back home. Bill and Kathy remained for the day, once again packing the car and the rental trailer, preparing for their move to Minnesota. The following day they too left, Bob went back to work and I was glad that I needed to pack for the move. Without the extra work to do, the quietness in our home would have been overwhelming.

We'd chosen to buy a duplex for our new home in Great Falls. The people who were living in the part we'd selected for our home were to be out of town for two weeks, and gave us permission to paint and carpet the entire home during that time. We worked the full time and completed everything except our bedroom during those two weeks. The bedroom would have to be done later.

We had three birthdays to celebrate in August; mine on the 15th, Bill's on the 20th and Kathy's on the 28th. We called Bill and Kathy on Bill's birthday and found Kathy was having a surprise party for him. We were happy to hear they had already used the golf clubs we'd given each of them for their birthdays.

When we called on Kathy's birthday we told them we would be loading the furniture the next day and the phone would be disconnected. We would talk with them again after our new phone was installed in Great Falls. Kathy mentioned that she would be getting her eyes examined September 3. She had worn glasses for years and we'd made it a policy of her to have an eye examination each summer. She wanted to have her test done in Minnesota so her eye doctor would be near her home. We said our goodbyes with joy—we knew they were happy in their new home and we would soon be in ours.

and the
Two
shall become
One

Our daughter, Kathryn Louise, and William F. Zastrow will be united in Christ on Sunday, the third of August, Nineteen hundred and seventy-five at three o'clock in the afternoon in the Saint Paul Lutheran Church, Lewistown, Montana.

You are invited to join in worship, witness their vows and share in the joy of the beginning of their new life together at the reception, buffet and wedding dance, in the Yogo Inn, following the ceremony.

If you are unable to attend, we ask your presence in thought and prayer.

Mr. and Mrs. Robert L. Joseph

Top Left: Getting those invitations out. Top Right: Engagement . Bottom Left: Finishing touches on those dresses. Bottom Right: Shower in Plevna.

Here comes the bride

Wedding Party

Cake cutting time

We danced the night away

VI

Moving day arrived. Our furniture was loaded on a truck, we spent the night in a motel in Lewistown and got an early start for Great Falls. We wanted to finish our painting before the moving van arrived.

September 3rd—our 25th Wedding Anniversary. Bob worked in Havre that day; I supervised the unloading of our furniture and started sorting through the boxes. Just as the movers were leaving, a floral arrangement from Reuben and Evelyn was delivered, followed shortly by Bob, home from Havre. He quickly finished his business; I got cleaned up, pinned on a rose from the bouquet and we went out, a tired but happy couple, to eat our anniversary dinner.

The following day our phone was installed. Almost immediately we had a call from Evelyn checking to see how the move had gone. No sooner had I finished talking with her than a second phone call came through—Kathy and Bill. Kathy broke the news. She had been in for her eye examination; the doctor found that she had lost most of the peripheral vision in one eye. He could see something on her optic nerve. He suspected a tumor and arranged for her to report to the Mayo Clinic immediately. She was already in Rochester when she phoned. Kathy tried to reassure me; her faith had not wavered. Once again she reminded me there was no need to worry.

The phone felt like it weighed a ton as I hung it up. A tumor—no need to worry?

I don't know when I've felt more alone or more helpless than I did at that moment. We hadn't lived in Great Falls long enough to have made friends or to have become a part of a church family. Bob was working in Lewistown that day. I had no one to turn to—no one except God, and all I could bring myself to do was ask questions. "Why?" "Why Kathy?" "How could this have happened?" "What did we do wrong?"

We had hired a carpenter to put up some shelves for us that day. He heard me crying and, respecting my privacy, left for the day. I called Lewistown, hoping to find Bob. He wasn't in; I left a message for him to return my call.

Taking that simple action brought some relief. I was able to pray—to reach out to God with more than questions. At that time, I felt great comfort in the knowledge that God knows the meaning of our deepest sighs. Pain too deep for words is understood perfectly by God and He can bring peace into even that anguish that we feel is unbearable.

The phone rang; Bob had gotten my message. Talking with Bob was calming. I was no longer alone with my fears. I'd turned some over to God; I'd shared some with Bob. I knew I was no longer alone.

Kathy and Bill didn't think it was necessary for us to go to Minnesota. They were confident everything would be fine. Bob called our pastor in Lewistown; I called Bob's family and mine. We felt the bond of mutual prayer with family and friends.

On September 11 Kathy had a CAT-scan. They called that evening to tell us she would be going home then, but would return to Rochester on the 14th for surgery on the 15th.

Once again Bob was working out of town; I called him that evening. We agreed that he should complete his calls quickly the next morning and get back to Great Falls as soon as possible. He called his boss and made arrangements for time off. He arrived in Great Falls at 2:30 the next afternoon. I had everything packed and ready to go, so we left immediately. We drove straight through, arriving at Kathy and Bill's the next afternoon.

Sunday we all went to Rochester. While Bill and Kathy went to the hospital, Bob and I found a place to stay. Our room was just a block from the hospital. The walk would be good for us.

That evening the doctor met with us in Kathy's room to explain the surgery. I had not realized her operation was considered brain surgery. As he described the procedure, my fears welled up inside.

My shock was apparent to the doctor. His touch was comforting as he reassured me, "It's OK, Mom. It's OK."

Kathy didn't want us to worry. I didn't want to upset her and yet I could no longer hold back my tears. I left the room. At my return, Kathy took my hand. "I heard you crying, Mom. I'll be OK. God will take care of me."

I knew she was right. If only I could have felt it the way she did! Instead, I just felt helpless. Bob and I kissed Kathy goodnight and walked to our room. Bill's sister lived in Rochester; his mother had come down to be with him. That was important for him.

The doctor had told us they would be taking Kathy to surgery early the next morning. We were there for a few moments of prayer before we watched them wheel her into the elevator. We hadn't had breakfast and, although none of us felt like eating, we knew we must keep our strength. Bill, Bob and I went out for a quick breakfast and hurried back to the waiting room in St. Mary's Hospital. In a room full of other families waiting for their loved ones to come from surgery, I felt alone. It was the helpless, sinking feeling with which I would become all too familiar in the days ahead.

Slowly the moments turned into hours. Time and again we would hear the intercom click on, we would strain to hear Kathy's name announced, and would slump back in our chairs as yet another family would be called out.

Noon came and went. Still we waited. The puzzles and cards scattered about the room were ignored. We would have another cup of coffee.

Finally, at 2:30, we were called to the recovery room. We were met by the doctor who told us the surgery had gone well; we could see Kathy in the Intensive Care Unit in about an hour.

It was about an hour and a half before we were called again and experienced, for the first time, a routine that would become a part of our lives as long as Kathy was in ICU. We could visit her for ten minutes every two hours, two people at a time.

Bill and I went in first. In the surgery, they had made an incision from ear to ear and lifted the skull to observe the tumor, taken a culture, and closed. I didn't know what to expect as I walked to her room. The relief at the sight of Kathy was overwhelming. My body shook with the flood of love I felt. Kathy opened her eyes. "Where's Daddy?"

She didn't know the visitation rules and felt we should all be together. I had seen her—that was all I needed for now. I left the room and sent Bob in to see her. He spent some time reassuring her with the doctor's words and sharing his faith in God's love and protective care. Then he, too, left, so Bill and Kathy could have a little time together. What a change from the laughing young couple at their wedding just six weeks earlier.

Throughout the day we called family and friends to report on Kathy's progress. We continued the visitation routine. Bill and I would go in first, then Bob, then Bill's mother, then other members of Bill's family as they arrived. The ten minutes would fly by. The two hours would drag on.

We returned to our room that night and continued our prayers—prayers that Kathy would not suffer, that the test results would be favorable. Our friends in Rochester, the Kelleys, called to say they would pray for Kathy in a special mass the next morning and would see us at the hospital the next night.

As soon as we awakened the next morning, we called the hospital. Kathy had had a good night.

Once again Bill and I were the first to go in for a visit. As we entered her room, we saw a crowd of doctors at the foot of her bed studying her chart. In panic, I hurried to the nurses' station. What could be wrong?

"Kathy is fine," the nurse reassured me. "But, Mrs. Joseph, Kathy has a very rare tumor. Those are interns studying her case."

From that moment on my fear intensified. Kathy would remind me that she was in God's hands. She would repeat again and again that, whatever happened, she would be fine. I knew that, too; I just couldn't stop worrying.

Kathy's roommate had also had surgery for a tumor. Through the following days we became friends. Janice was married and had two children. Her mother and I could understand and appreciate each other's concerns.

Kathy's day went well. Not surprisingly, she complained of a headache. The doctor gave Bill the news we'd hoped for. The tumor was benign. We thanked God that there was no cancer.

That evening as we left the hospital, we found the Kelleys and Denisons waiting for us. These were two of the men who, years before, had befriended Bob in Germany as he waited for news of the birth of his child. They had come again to listen, to care, to encourage, and comfort. We found a coffee shop and had a long, much-needed visit. True friends are a marvelous gift from God.

After a night's sleep, we quickly dressed and hurried to the hospital for our first visit of the day. We were pleased with Kathy's progress. She had always recovered quickly from any illness. This was the first surgery she'd had since she had her tonsils removed at five years of age.

As Kathy continued to improve, we began to relax. We were thankful that Janice continued to improve also.

That afternoon Kathy was moved from ICU to a private room. I didn't want her to be alone in her room that night and asked the doctor for permission to stay with her. He made the necessary arrangements, even offering to order a cot brought in for me. That wasn't necessary. There was a comfortable chair in the room; I would be happy just being close in case Kathy needed anything.

Bob and I went out for a bite to eat. We walked to our room so I could get my pillow and went back to the hospital. Bob and Bill said their good-nights, and Kathy quickly went to sleep. She slept soundly until the nurses came in around three o-clock to adjust the IV's.

Kathy couldn't get back to sleep. She was in pain. All the tubes restricted her movement so I was glad I was there to call the nurse for her. She was given a pain pill and soon she and I were asleep for the night.

We both awoke when the doctor came in to make his rounds. He reassured me—Kathy was doing fine, but he prescribed more sleep for me.

Telling Kathy I would return soon, I left to let Bob know how the night had gone. I quickly showered, changed clothes, and joined Bob for breakfast. We stopped in to see Kathy for a few moments. Then, in order to give Kathy and Bill some time alone, we went to make some more phone calls. Kathy's progress was so amazing, we could finally relax—at least enough to notice what a beautiful city Rochester is in the fall. The tree-lined streets were dressed in beautiful fall foliage. The Creator was reminding us once again of His unending presence. We felt His peace around us.

We had to be careful when we phoned my mother. She would get upset if we would say that Kathy had brain surgery; she thought that meant Kathy was deranged. My sister was able to help. She had a friend who was a nurse and was able to explain the surgery more clearly.

The news of Kathy's surgery was in the Lewistown paper, and soon she was receiving flowers and cards from her many friends. A nurse brought in a long string, fastened it on the wall, and we were able to display Kathy's cards around the room.

Day by day we could see Kathy's improvement. Near the end of the week, Bob knew it was time for him to return to Montana. His customers would be wondering where he was. On Sunday Bill, too, had to return home to get back to his job. I was glad I was able to stay with Kathy. We would visit when she was awake, and I was able to get caught up on my correspondence while she napped. The mail continued to pour in.

Kathy was discharged from the hospital on September 24. Bill would come to Rochester for us as soon as he could get away from school. Kathy was hungry for chicken. There was a restaurant across the street from the hospital that featured chicken dinners so we went there for lunch. It seemed like old times. As Kathy was growing up, whenever we would eat out she would order chicken. We had often joked about it.

"You know, Mom, the chicken tastes just like the Pepsi." The disappointment was apparent in Kathy's voice. During the surgery, some nerves had been stretched too far. Kathy's senses of taste and smell were gone and would not return. For a moment she was depressed. Then she remembered, Bill would be coming soon. The depression lifted; her eyes sparkled. She thought of Bill, and she was fine.

Thankful to be home, Kathy was determined not to let this problem change her life. The day after she got home from the hospital, we fixed lunch for some of Bill's co-workers. Kathy would nap for a while each afternoon so she would be rested when Bill got home. She attended a football game that weekend and was in church on Sunday morning.

Kathy had been home for a week when it was time to return to Rochester. She and Janice were scheduled to receive X-ray treatments Monday through Friday, returning to their homes for the weekend. This schedule was to be repeated for eight weeks.

The first week of the new routine, I went to Rochester with them. We had rented a room there, and Kathy spent her days writing thank-you notes for their wedding gifts. It had been two months since the wedding, and those people who didn't know about the surgery were beginning to wonder if their gifts had arrived. Over and over Kathy wrote of her ordeal. Finally the notes were completed, and the weekend had arrived. We returned to Winthrop, did the laundry, cleaned the house, and I knew it was time for me to say good-bye. Kathy and Bill could manage on their own. It was time for me to get home to Bob and organize our new home. I'd been gone for eight weeks and had boxes needing to be unpacked. Bill and Kathy took me to Wilmar, Minnesota to catch a train home.

Janice and Kathy took turns driving to Rochester. They became very good friends , sharing their fears, their worries, and their joys. Kathy also had an opportunity to get to know Bill's family better, as she often stayed with them overnight and met Janice at Mankato to drive to Rochester together for their week of treatments.

Kathy could always find something to be thankful for in every situation. These new friendships were the silver lining on the cloud of illness.

We needed to see Kathy's progress and planned to spend Christmas with her and Bill. In the mean time, Kathy phoned and wrote regularly. She never complained. We missed her confiding in us but were happy that she had a husband with whom she could share her concerns.

Their home was decorated beautifully for Christmas. They had a large artificial tree that looked real and had adorned their stairway railing with large red and green bows. Their home reflected their love and hope and their faith in God.

It was great to see Kathy looking quite healthy. Her hair had begun to grow out, but with the Minnesota winter weather, she enjoyed wearing her wigs.

Christmas Day we went to church, then to Good Thunder for dinner and the afternoon with Bill's family. All too soon it was time for us to return to Montana. Just before we left, Bill and Kathy took us to St. Paul to the conservatory. Knowing I love plants, they had planned this as a parting gift for me. It was beautifully decorated with poinsettias, green plants, and blooming flowers of all kinds. A beautiful contrast to the winter weather outside.

Bob had saved a week of vacation to visit his family. Bill and Kathy came from Minnesota, my mother traveled with us, and we all enjoyed Easter in Nebraska. We were concerned at Kathy's thin, pale appearance, but she assured us she felt good.

Not long after our return home, we received a call from Kathy and Bill. They were selling their home and moving to Seward for a year. Bill would enroll at Concordia Teachers College to become a Director of Christian Education. When Bill and Kathy had married, he had promised her that within one year he would decide if he intended to continue working in public schools or return to school to prepare for church work. They had made the arrangements on their Easter trip but hadn't wanted to say anything until they had all the details worked out.

The school year was over; the house had been sold. They loaded their belongings into a rental truck and drove to Nebraska. Friends and relatives helped them get settled in. Then Bill and Kathy drove north for a short vacation.

During Kathy's years of teaching in Minnesota, she'd had a chance to become familiar with Bill's home state; she was eager to show Montana to him. She also had fond memories of visiting relatives in Canada so we decided to take a short trip to Canada and return to Great Falls via Glacier Park. Kathy marvelled at the artistry of God and the love He's shown us by creating such majestic beauty for us to enjoy. She was quick to point out the variety of gentle, fragile wild flowers amid the towering peaks, plunging water falls and roaring rivers. She loved sharing God's beauty with Bill and us.

July saw Bill and Kathy returning to their apartment in Nebraska. For Kathy it was a homecoming. Much of the staff at CTC was unchanged, and Bill was soon enjoying visits to Grandma's house with Kathy. Returning to the campus was like a step back in time, only this time Kathy could share it all with Bill.

Because she had no brothers or sisters, Kathy treasured close relationships with her cousins. She had included each of them in her wedding and wanted to attend each of their weddings as well. Her cousin Wanda was married in Baker, Montana in August that year.

I went to my sister's a few days early to help her prepare for the wedding. As we were readying the church basement, I couldn't help but wish Kathy could have come. I understood the situation. They'd just driven from Montana to Nebraska, and Bill was busy with school. They needed to stay in Seward, but....

My sister called me to the phone. It was Kathy. They'd just arrived at my brother's. Everyone else had known they were coming, but they'd all kept it a secret from me. What a joyous surprise! We enjoyed our brief visit, and Kathy had made it to one more wedding.

With Kathy gone and Bob's job keeping him on the road much of the time, I started taking a more active part in church activities. I loved it. Soon I was the Montana Mission Service Chairman for Lutheran Women's Missionary League (LWML).

That fall I had a meeting to attend in St. Louis. Bob took some vacation time, and we flew first to Dallas to visit my brother and his family, then to St. Louis for the meeting, and finally to Lincoln, Nebraska where Kathy and Bill met us and took us to Seward. I was glad to see their apartment; it was important to me to be able to picture her in her home as I read her letters and talked with her on the phone.

Kathy looked good and said she was feeling fine. She was very proud of Bill and was pleased that she was able to work to help with the finances. She was a substitute school teacher, waitress, and baby-sitter. She considered any job important for each one presented opportunities to witness to others about God.

Bill and Kathy came to Great Falls for Christmas. It was necessary for them to change planes in Denver. As they boarded the plane for the final leg of their journey, they could not find their tickets. The airline held the flight as Bill hurried back to the plane they'd just left. No tickets! Frontier Airlines helped them quickly make arrangements to continue their flight. The tickets had been purchased with a credit card; when the loss was reported, the full price of the tickets was refunded. From then on, we purchased all our travel tickets with a credit card.

Bill was to have his first experience with a warm chinook wind that Christmas. We awoke one morning and found twelve inches of snow on the ground. That afternoon the chinook came, the temperature shot up quickly, and by evening, all the snow was melted. Bill, like many people from other areas who are used to snow staying for months, was amazed as he stood watching the snow turn into rivulets as though blasted by a furnace, a familiar sight for people who live in Montana.

Their visit was typical of many to come. My mother came from Billings to spend some time with them. We all enjoyed playing games and nearly every evening would find us playing some game. One by one, as we got tired, we would drift off to bed. Bob and Kathy were still night owls and would often sit up together talking long after everyone else was in bed.

Winter was nearly over when we received a phone call from Bozeman, Montana. Friends who live there called to say their congregation had decided to call a Director of Christian Education. "Could you talk Bill into coming?"

We laughed. We would not have tried to influence Bill's decisions even if we did think we could. We were happy to give our friends Bill's address and phone number; and I couldn't help but dream of the possibility. Bozeman is just 179 miles from Great Falls; that would be close enough to see each other frequently, but far enough apart to enjoy our separate lives.

In a matter of weeks, Bill told us on the phone, "I was in Montana last weekend. I have a call to Bozeman." We were thrilled. Just 179 miles away. Bill would serve his internship in Kansas City as the final step in his training, then they would move to Montana. We praised God for His wonderful love.

Bill had been selected as a member of the Concordia Singers. Kathy had enjoyed that experience so much she was thrilled for him; however, that meant he would be on the Spring Tour over Easter vacation. Bob's mother hadn't been to our new home, so we had Kathy and Grandma fly to Great Falls for Easter. My mother came, too, as well as a cousin from Canada, and we celebrated our Saviour's Resurrection together.

First Home & Christmas

Home in Montana for
Christmas 1976

Kathy & Martha at
convention
"took Mom to hospital"

2nd Anniversary

Deb, Jerl's Wedding;
in charge of guest book

VII

Our friends, the Martels, found a house for Bill and Kathy, and by the middle of August, they were on their way to Montana. On August 21, 1977, Bill was installed as the D.C.E. at First Lutheran Church in Bozeman. Kathy was very proud of her husband and expressed her thankfulness to God for His kindness to them.

Happy days followed. Bill was perfectly suited to church work, and Kathy loved serving by his side. During their time in Bozeman, both grew in their service to the Lord. Kathy enjoyed substitute teaching occasionally, was active in Sunday School, Children's Choir, Bible Study, and often accompanied Bill on his hospital and shut-in calls. They both had beautiful voices and would often sing duets as a part of the devotions Bill conducted with the shut-ins. Bill was responsible for many of the activities the church conducted for a group of mentally retarded people that worshipped at First Lutheran. Kathy joined him in this work, and a strong mutual love grew between Bill and Kathy and the group. Kathy and Bill had an abundance of patience and would openly demonstrate their affection—attributes needed for that work. Bill's position allowed him to perform a variety of other responsibilities as well. Kathy and Bill and their home glowed with love for God and His people.

Both Bill and Kathy were involved with the Children's Christmas Service that year and invited us to spend Christmas in Bozeman with them. They would then come to Great Falls for New Year's Eve and Day. There was a touch of sadness that Christmas. We received a letter from Janice's mother. Janice had died on August 21. Kathy remembered the time they had shared when they were receiving X-ray treatments in Rochester. It was a sobering letter. Our hearts ached for Janice's family and her mother. We thanked God anew for the gift of Kathy's life.

Miles City had been chosen as the host society for the LWML Montana District Convention that spring. Kathy and I had been invited to stay with Marcia, whose husband worked for the same company as Bob. As we were registering, a woman walked up to us to introduce herself.

"Ever since I heard Mrs. Joseph was coming," she said, "I've been waiting to meet you." She was Mrs. Hazel Witcher. Twenty-five years before, we had lived in the same home while waiting for our babies to be born. There were several of us women who lived too far away from the hospital to stay at home until our labor started so there was a home in town where we could spend those last days. Hazel had been there when it was time for Kathy to be born. She'd carried my suitcase to the hospital for me and had admitted me. I had never seen her again until that day at the convention. In the years since then, this relationship has brought peace and comfort to me.

We saw Kathy and Bill quite often and really couldn't notice any change in her condition. Every six months, she had to report for a checkup; one appointment each year would be in Billings and the other in Rochester. One doctor did detect a change in the tumor which caused a further loss of vision in her left eye. She was no longer allowed to drive.

Summers were busy for both of our families. Bob took orders for Christmas merchandise in the summer, and Bill and Kathy would be involved in many youth activities. With the three birthdays and one anniversary in August, we would try to get together a few times.

In September of 1978, we met Kathy and Bill in Baker to travel together to Nebraska to Kathy's cousin Jerl and Deb's wedding. We enjoyed a visit with Bob's Mother. She had missed Bill and Kathy after they moved to Bozeman.

As Bill and Kathy became more involved in their congregation, they had less time available for trips to Great Falls. Bill often conducted the worship services at Ennis and Three Forks. On those Sundays when the pastor would conduct Communion Service at Ennis and Three Forks, Bill would lead the worship in Bozeman. Kathy usually accompanied Bill wherever he was leading the worship. Occasionally, weather permitting, they would continue on from Three Forks to Great Falls for an overnight visit with us. When we did see Kathy, we were pleased that she continued to look healthy and was always in a very happy mood.

We enjoyed a visit from them that February when Bill was responsible for part of the program for a church youth gathering in Great Falls. It was exciting to see how the young people would respond to Bill and Kathy.

By fall Bill and Kathy had moved. First Lutheran was without a minister at the time, and the congregation wanted Bill and Kathy to move into the parsonage so Bill would be closer to the church.

When Kathy went for her checkup in Rochester, Bill took some of his vacation time, and they visited with his family and friends. They celebrated their birthdays there. We were relieved when they told us the check up had gone well. Bill and Kathy did not like to discuss her health with others so we learned few of the details included in the doctors' reports.

Bob's mother's birthday is November 3rd, and that year she was celebrating her eighty-eighth. Bill and I had too many church commitments to leave, so Bob and Kathy decided to travel together. They both flew to Denver (Bob from Great Falls and Kathy from Bozeman) and met there for the flight to Nebraska. They had a great time together, but Bob was very concerned when Kathy had a serious reaction to her medication.

Bill was still the only D.C.E. in Montana. As such, he was expected to attend the District Pastoral Conferences. Consequently, we were excited to learn that a February meeting for the pastors would be held in Great Falls. We knew Kathy would accompany Bill. Our excitement multiplied when we learned that Kathy and Bill would attend a meeting with Lutheran Social Services that same weekend. That meeting was the first step in preparing to adopt a child through L.S.S.

The weekend finally arrived. While Bill was in meetings, Kathy and I shopped. We looked at cribs and baby clothes and all the little things a new baby needs. We looked and dreamed and planned.

Bill and Kathy stayed at the Ursuline Academy, the meeting's location, overnight. But when they had a short break in the evening, they walked to our house. The thought of a baby had them walking on clouds. Their meeting was great! The seminar was great! The world was great! They could hardly contain their joy.

The end of the month we phoned to see how things were going. Kathy wasn't feeling well. She and Bill and a friend had been grocery shopping earlier that evening. Probably because of the loss of her peripheral vision, Kathy had walked into a pole in the store. She was in a great deal of pain. Her doctor was out of town, and Bill and Kathy hadn't found anything to relieve her headache.

Bob had a meeting to attend in Billings; but as soon as the sales meeting concluded, we drove to Bozeman. Kathy still felt sick. She could be up for just a few moments before she needed to lie down and rest again. She thought perhaps she would feel better if she ate. She wanted to go out to eat, thinking the fresh air would help her feel better. She seemed to enjoy her meal; but as soon as she got home, she went to bed. We'd done all we could and thought she might rest better if we went on home. She didn't need to be thinking about being a hostess at that time.

We called to check on Kathy several times that weekend. Finally Bill had heard from the doctor. Kathy was to report to the hospital in Billings on March 3rd. On the fourth, they would implant a shunt in her head to drain fluid from her brain into her intestine. The pressure would be relieved and the headaches solved.

As we sat in the waiting room, anxious for a message from the doctor, I kept remembering the first surgery—the long hours of waiting. This operation required less time. Kathy's recuperative powers were surprising; she was in the Intensive Care Unit just a few days. Most of her eyesight was gone. She could distinguish light from dark, that was all.

We took Kathy home from the hospital on March 13th, knowing she would return on the twenty-fourth for yet another operation. I went home with Bill and Kathy to help care for Kathy and to do some of the household chores. Kathy needed to build up her strength for the coming surgery.

Bill, Kathy, and I went to a musical presented by students she had taught. Kathy was unable to see them, but Bill described the action and she knew the music by memory. Following their performances, the students came down into the audience to give Kathy hugs and to receive her words of praise.

News of the impending surgery and its seriousness had spread throughout the community, the family, and the church. Prayers on Kathy's behalf were offered across the country. This was the most serious surgery Kathy had faced yet.

We were there by six o'clock the morning of the surgery. They would be removing the tumor in a few hours and, with it, Kathy's optic nerve. She would be blind. The nurse had shaved her head; Kathy had comforted us with her confession of faith, quoting Scripture to remind us that God is in control. All would be well. We kissed her, watched them take her, and then we waited.

——Yes, that day would be different for us. This time we had family with us. Bill's folks were there. My sister Delphine and sisters-in-law Phyllis and Vivian sat with us. My mother stayed at home to care for Vivian's little girl. The hours dragged by. There was coffee in the room; none of us even thought of needing to eat. We stayed and waited. We paced and prayed.

At last the doctor entered the room and called Bill, Bob, and me aside.

"The tumor was about the size of a lemon," he began. "I'm sorry, the tumor is just too close to the brain for us to remove it entirely."

Oh no! After all she'd been through, all the pain yet to come, the tumor was still there! The doctor was still talking. What did he say?

His words shattered the air and echoed through my head. "The tumor is malignant."

We stood stunned. We had pushed the dreaded word "cancer" from our minds, but there it was confronting us head on. There it was, invading Kathy's life.

A question blasted through my shocked mind. I struggled to stifle it. I couldn't—I needed to know! "How long does she have to live?"

"Eighteen months to two years."

Eighteen months. Two years. But she's only twenty-seven years old. Just weeks before we had been shopping for a crib. She had so much to live for. So much to give.

Eighteen months to two years.

My struggle entered a new phase that day. I had worried about Kathy's eyesight, and I had hated a tumor; but I had continued to hope and to dream. I had hoped for the continuation of what seemed to be a recovery; I had dreamed of a baby in their home.

That day worry about her eyesight ended. She was blind—with her optic nerve gone, there was no hope that she would ever see again. Thoughts of a grandchild were dashed. My enemy carried a new name, "cancer". I was determined not to let Kathy see my despair. I would encourage her.

Kathy, too, had a new struggle on her hands. She must learn to deal with the blindness. She had "practiced" being blind. Knowing she would be losing her eyesight, she had tried to iron with her eyes closed. She had practiced walking through her home with her eyes closed. The dress rehearsal was over. The real struggle had begun.

Examining Braille
Miles City Convention

28 years old

5th Anniversary

Blind Kathy in
her kitchen (left)

Blind, learning to use recorder and cane

VIII

Having attended Pastoral Conferences and youth meetings throughout the state with Bill, Kathy was known by all our church's ministers in Montana. One of those ministers was a patient in the same hospital at that time, having suffered a serious stroke. Each minister that went to the hospital to visit him would stop to visit Kathy also. At times there were so many in her room that Bob and I had to go to the waiting room. The hospital staff recognized Kathy's need for rest and put a sign on her door restricting company to family only. That stopped everyone except the ministers.

As Kathy improved, she eagerly welcomed the return of other guests, especially classmates from her years as a student at Trinity Lutheran School. They'd remained friends throughout the years.

One of the first problems Kathy faced because of her blindness was her inability to recognize the time of day. Her world was one constant shade of darkness, and when she would awaken, she wouldn't know if it was night or day. We had promised to check on a watch for her, when, much to our surprise, a man brought a braille watch to her—a gift from Zale's Jewelers. With a brief lesson, she could read the time; a major frustration had been removed.

Kathy was released from the hospital in time to celebrate Easter at home. A large banner was hung in anticipation of her arrival. The mentally retarded people with whom Bill and Kathy had worked had made it for her. In bold letters it proclaimed "God Loves You and So Do We." Each person's name was printed on a heart. Unable to see it, Kathy felt it lovingly, knowing the effort required to make it. Bill

80

described it in detail as Kathy touched it. It was then displayed above the arched entrance to their dining room for all their guests to see.

Bill's work was beginning to pile up; Kathy didn't want him to neglect his responsibilities. My mother provided the perfect answer. She was free to go to Bozeman and help Kathy. It would take some time for Kathy to adjust to her blindness, and Grandma was a patient helper. She remembered when Kathy's patient help had made it possible for her to be in her own home. She was glad she would have a chance to help Kathy.

First Lutheran members demonstrated their Christian love with a steady procession of food. Full meals were delivered to Bill and Kathy's. Several fund raisers were sponsored to help Kathy and Bill cover their medical expenses. Love was shown in many little ways as well: company on a walk, fresh garden produce to eat, and a homemade stuffed elephant for the menagerie in Kathy's spare bedroom. Love flowed into their home from all their friends and back to the friends from Kathy and Bill.

The following article, entitled "Young Woman Faces Blindness with Courage", by Joan Haines the Features Editor, appeared in the Bozeman *Chronicle* of April 27, 1980.

Kathy Zastrow has been blind for three weeks, and she says it's a challenge. It's a challenge she's determined to meet and conquer.

Kathy became totally blind following an operation in March in which a tumor was removed from beneath her brain. Her optic nerve, wound around the tumor, was also taken out.

Now, four weeks later, she moves around her home carefully but with determination. She shares her home, the parsonage of the First Lutheran Church in Bozeman, with her husband Bill, who's in charge of the church's youth education program.

She's dressed comfortably in slacks, her head wrapped in a colorful bandana which covers the white bandages which encircle her head. When she walks from one room to another, she reaches in front of her with her hands, tapping the air gently to keep from running into obstacles.

Many times Kathy wondered what it would be like to be blind.

"There's a big difference between closing my eyes, trying to understand blindness, and standing here with my eyes open, not being able to see," she said.

Her husband Bill says he keeps forgetting his wife is blind.

"He tells me something is over here or over there, and I have to ask him where here or there is," she said.

Sometimes when the furniture, such as her rocking chair, is moved several inches from its former position, she gets confused. Bill often tries to help her get oriented, as he did in their living room midweek.

"Don't help me, don't help me," Kathy said. "I know where I am now. Don't help me."

In 1975, one month after she and Bill were married, Kathy found out she had optic glioma, a tumor entwined in her optic nerve under her brain. An operation was performed to find out if the tumor was benign. It was. Kathy underwent radiation treatments. The tumor seemed to go into remission.

In 1978, Kathy's neuro-surgeon, Lashman Soriya of Billings, told her the tumor was in a new stage of growth. This year he said two operations would have to be performed.

On March 3, a shunt was implanted in her head. A shunt is a device that relieves pressure on the brain by draining fluid from the brain into the abdomen. On March 25, the tumor and optic nerve were removed.

The tumor was found to be malignant. Because it was located so close to the brain, it wasn't possible to remove the entire growth. Kathy and Bill will be traveling to San Francisco, where Kathy will undergo another operation and more treatments to remove the growth.

Following the first operation, Kathy could only distinguish the shading of light, from bright to dark. After the second, she saw nothing at all.

Following each operation, friends found her sitting in her hospital bed attempting to type. At her house, she placed adhesive tape on her typewriter's four "home" typewriter keys, a, f, j, and colon, to make it easier to type accurately.

Kathy irons, sets the table, vacuums, and does the laundry. She practiced ironing before she went blind by performing the task with her eyes closed.

"I start with the collar, go to the sleeves, then go on to the front and back of the shirt. With trousers, I match up the seams before ironing. That's no problem," Kathy said.

She and Bill do the cooking together.

"We fixed soup and sandwiches for our first meal after I got home from the hospital," Kathy said. "It took one hour."

When she vacuums, she pushes the vacuum in one direction. She's afraid she'll knock something over if she pushes it back and forth.

Before the operations, Kathy taught music as a substitute teacher for the Bozeman public schools. She also gave private piano lessons. She gave her last lesson March 1.

She still plays the piano. She knows her favorite songs by heart.

After working with personnel employed by Visual Rehabilitation Services who visit her from Helena, she's hoping to continue to teach.

She's using her teaching ability now. She directs the junior choir at the First Lutheran Church.

A tape recorder and record player from the Montana state library bring books and bluegrass into Kathy's life. A braille watch given to her by Zale's Jewelry allows her to tell time.

A visit with a blind student at Montana State University, Floyd Smithson, helped Bill learn how to lead Kathy properly when she takes his arm.

"I learned to talk with my elbow," Bill said. "For instance, I put my arm back and down to signal that Kathy should stop."

Kathy was excited at midweek because visual rehabilitation services counselor, Lynne Lee, had brought her a collapsible cane.

"Oh terrific," she said. "I've been waiting for this. I'll probably wipe out all the furniture in the process of using it."

The counselor helped her stretch out and collapse the lightweight cane. She had trouble collapsing it after the counselor left.

"Can I help you?" asked Bill.

"No," said Kathy. "You won't always be with me."

"I'll probably get it all broken in and then you'll say, 'Gee, this is easy.'"

Kathy's strong faith in God has helped her to face her blindness with courage.

"I know God is with us," she said. "He promised He won't give us more than we can bear. Nobody knows how many years the Lord will have me live. The best thing for me to do is to put on a positive smile."

We went to Bozeman to spend Memorial Day weekend. Kathy had her cane by then, and she was very happy. That weekend Bill and Kathy flew to San Francisco for another operation.

I sat watching Kathy for a time that weekend, marvelling at how she could be so happy after all she'd been through. I wondered how much more she could take.

She knew she couldn't live with the cancer: It could not be surgically removed, and she'd had all the radiation and chemotherapy her body could tolerate. This was the only treatment recommended for her. She would be the thirty-second person to have radium beads implanted in her head, performed in that hospital.

They called us after surgery, and they were very pleased with her progress. Once again Kathy's strong recuperative powers were exercised. They took time to see a little bit of San Francisco and returned to Bozeman around Father's Day.

Bill and Kathy had usually come to Great Falls for both Mothers' Day and Fathers' Day. That year we gladly went to Bozeman to see them. Kathy was most comfortable in her own home, and we were just thankful to see them—we didn't care where we got together.

For some time Kathy had been having trouble with her fluid balance. She was always thirsty and yet she retained fluids. In San Francisco, they'd found a medicine that helped her. In order to get the medicine in Montana, it had to be ordered in—a six-month supply at a time. We were thankful a drug store would order it for her. It took her some time to get used to the medication; it had to be inhaled by nose.

Neatness had been one of Kathy's strong characteristics all her life. When she lost her sight, the orderliness became even more important. Everything had to be in place or she would waste much of her time just looking for things. She had always kept her kitchen cabinets precisely arranged; therefore, even though she was blind, she was able to find exactly what she wanted with very little trouble.

Kathy continued to take part in the Wednesday Bible Study, and those women provided a strong support group for her. Some of them spent several days in Kathy's home, helping her glue braille tags to her lotion, cosmetics, and medicine jars. They sewed braille color identification labels to her towels and washcloths so she could read which ones matched.

A letter from a member of that Bible Study group reveals how important the group and Kathy were to each other.

Kathy was truly an inspiration to all of us here at First Lutheran. And especially at our Wednesday afternoon Bible study. She knew the Bible so well, and when most of us would be stumped for an answer, Kathy would come up with it for us. When we were studying a book called "The Life of St. Paul" by W. Arndt, D.D., Ph.D., we had a large map on the wall. As we talked and discussed his journeys and traced them on the map, Kathy would stand up and tell one of us to take her hand and move it along the map so she could know about the journeys also. We would give her the mile gauge with her fingers.

I remember several weeks when three or four of us went home with Kathy after our Bible Study. We were sewing the Braille tags for colors on her clothes. She stood by the closet and selected the clothes she wanted marked and explained the Braille tags to us. It was a fun time for all of us.

Kathy wanted to live so very much and serve others which she did with a loving, strong faith in God.

One Wednesday afternoon we heard Kathy coming to the basement room of the church where we met. And she got mixed up because the chairs that usually were against the wall had been moved. She was so frustrated that she threw her cane to the floor and started to cry. We all took turns to hug her and to tell her it was okay. In a matter of minutes, she was her sweet, pleasant

self again, and we went on with our Bible study. This was
shortly after Kathy became blind.

We are all so much richer having known Kathy—we speak
of her very often, and I'll always remember Kathy.

In Christ, Irene "Mickey" Jesswein

The following article appeared in a Lutheran Women's
Missionary League *Quarterly:*

Evelyn Lyons has been deaf from birth, Kathy Zastrow
became blind after a recent brain tumor operation. Both are
members of the Bible class at First Lutheran, Bozeman, MT.

Evelyn always studies her lesson before class and her
thoughtful preparation contributes a great deal to the class's
understanding of the lesson. Members of the class assist her by
writing down the discussion as it takes place during class.

Bill's parents came to Montana to spend some time with Kathy
and Bill, and his mother helped Kathy with labeling items. We were
all amazed at the many aids that have been developed to make life
more comfortable and convenient for blind people. These aids make
it possible for blind persons to be quite independent.

In July Kathy and Bill were counselors at a church youth camp.
Kathy also provided some music—she loved to lead singing in a
choir or around a campfire. The young people couldn't help but
notice that Kathy's faith and joy were undaunted by her blindness.

In August we drove to Bozeman to celebrate Kathy and Bill's
Fifth Wedding Anniversary with them. Kathy's cousin Lois, who
had been Kathy's maid of honor, was there also. She brought a
porch swing for Kathy and Bill. It was a gift they would enjoy on
many summer evenings. The day was difficult for Kathy. She was
struggling with her emotions; so much had happened in those five
years and so many of their dreams had been destroyed. By evening
she had gained control. Her self-pity conquered, she was thankful,
once again, for the blessings she did have. I never saw her depressed
again.

That night I recalled praying years before for God to send Kathy someone special. Just how special Bill was would become increasingly apparent. He had tremendous patience with Kathy—and she with him. Whenever being in a strange setting would upset Kathy, he knew exactly how to make her feel comfortable. Whenever their problems would become depressing for Bill, her faith would bolster his, and they would both be encouraged.

Bill knew it was important for Kathy to stay busy. He continued to take her with him on shut-in calls; after her blindness, her singing meant even more to the people they visited. Her continued cheerfulness was an inspiration to many.

Bill's birthday occurred during the fall Pastor-Teacher Conference being held in Bozeman that year. During the conference, the pastors and teachers presented Kathy and Bill with a tandem bike. Bill and Kathy had looked at the bicycle-built-for-two before she was blind, so Kathy knew exactly what it looked like. Biking was a favorite activity of theirs since the days when they had dated. Although Kathy found it hard to relax on the bike because of her blindness, she was thrilled with the wind in her face and the chance for exercise. Many evenings they could be seen "cruising" the streets.

Bob and I knew a woman who did brailling for the church, so we mailed Kathy's birthday card to Evelyn to have the message brailled for Kathy. She was so excited about being able to read her card that she phoned us immediately to thank us. A brailled message seemed like a nice touch to us; to Kathy it was tremendously important. Her deep appreciation of a simple act like the ability to read made us aware of how much we take for granted.

It had taken just a few visits for Kathy to become comfortable in our home again. During one of her visits, a neighbor of ours and his daughter came over. Jenny began asking Kathy questions about her blindness. In answering the questions, Kathy found an opportunity to talk about God.

"You must remember that my blindness is not a punishment. God isn't punishing me or my parents or my husband. Because of sin, there is suffering here on earth; because of sin, there is blindness. But when we believe in Jesus Christ for our salvation, then all of our sins are forgiven. Some day I'll be in heaven with my

Lord and then I will have a perfect body—no more tears or pain or blindness.

John thanked Kathy for talking with Jenny, for patiently answering her questions. He appreciated Kathy's openness. Kathy hadn't stopped to consider whether or not she should talk about God. There was never any question in her mind. She just always witnessed in a most relaxed and natural way.

Traveling became more difficult for Kathy. Her medicine had to be kept chilled, and it was frustrating for her to find her way around in a strange place. Yet she wouldn't pass up the chance to attend a cousin's wedding.

In October, my brother Arnold's oldest son, Craig, was married to Wanda. We went to Bozeman and picked up Bill and Kathy; then on to Laurel where I stayed for a meeting while the rest attended the wedding in Baker.

We went to Bozeman for Thanksgiving. Bill and Kathy had smoked a turkey and then cooked it on their grill. Although Bill cooked the turkey, he was careful to let Kathy feel that she had a part in it. She did quite well in the kitchen, insisting on her independence as much as possible. She prepared the rest of the meal, allowing me to assist only slightly.

Kathy always wanted to do her part. She and Bill had been invited to dinner by a family from First Lutheran. While Bill was outside with the husband, Kathy offered to set the table. Later when she heard the hostess move one of the plates a little, Kathy asked anxiously, "What's the matter? Did I do something wrong?"

It was frustrating to just watch when Kathy was having trouble with something, but we knew she would be unhappy if we helped too much. Kathy did not want to be pampered.

Later Bill and Kathy bought a microwave oven, which was a great help. Kathy would prepare the food as much as she could in the afternoon, and Bill could cook it quickly when he got home.

Early in December Kathy took a two-week course to help her increase her mobility. Bill drove her to Missoula where I would stay with her. While Kathy was attending classes, a counselor talked with me about my understanding and acceptance of Kathy's condition. I understood that at any time the radium beads could begin to attack the healthy cells in Kathy's brain. I knew that at any moment she could die. My faith made it possible for me to accept that.

That weekend I learned from watching the counselors with Kathy that I was over-protective. They took Kathy walking so she could practice learning to use her cane. At one point she veered into the street. I wanted to grab her, to call to her; but with just a word, the counselor calmly directed Kathy back onto the sidewalk. The added mobility was very important to independent Kathy.

That Christmas Kathy sang in her last concert. The Bozeman Symphonic Choir presented Handel's *Messiah*. Kathy learned the entire cantata by memory and was thrilled when the choir asked her to sing with them. The woman standing next to her would touch her elbow to signal their entrances and cuts. Kathy's spirit soared with their voices.

Joan Haines wrote another article about Kathy that December.

Kathy Zastrow has been blind for less than a year, but on Thanksgiving she was thankful. As Christmas approaches, she says she has so much to be happy about.

"I'm grateful to be alive," said Kathy, who had a brain tumor and optic nerve removed last March 25.

The tumor was located so close to the brain that it wasn't possible to remove the entire growth. The tumor was found to be malignant.

So Kathy and her husband Bill traveled to San Francisco last June, where radium seeds were implanted near the core of the tumor by Dr. Phillip Gutin. The radium seeds acted on the tissues surrounding the core.

When Kathy returned to San Francisco in October, examination by a catscanner showed that the tumor core had been reduced 50 percent since the operation, an experimental procedure performed on only 34 people.

That's one of the things she's grateful for.

She's also happy because she's improved her mobility and her ability to perform many household tasks.

For twelve days this month, she attended a workshop in Missoula designed to improve living skills. The workshop was sponsored by the Montana Visual Services Department.

Kathy worked on improving her food preparation abilities, preparing soups and salads.

She and her instructor Donna Mathis worked on Kathy's ability to get around outdoors.

"I crossed a busy intersection in Missoula by myself," she said. "I listened to the traffic noises. When the parallel traffic started, I began to cross the street."

Kathy also walked to a post office in Missoula and bought a stamp.

She received instruction on how to walk safely on a snowy sidewalk. "I'm supposed to push my cane down hard through the snow to make sure there's sidewalk underneath."

Kathy is working on becoming more proficient in braille. She learned the language when she attended a summer school workshop at Montana State University taught by the Montana Association for the Blind. She's able to type braille on a typewriter borrowed from the Visual Services Department in Helena.

Kathy's husband, Bill, is youth education director of the First Lutheran Church. A friend of theirs dictated all the names and numbers of church members onto a tape. Kathy will type the names and numbers on her braille typewriter, making a phone book for her own use.

This past weekend, Kathy and Bill have been especially busy. They both sang with the Bozeman Symphony Chorus for the performance of the "Messiah." They decorated their Christmas tree.

Kathy will be attending the Christmas party of the Gallatin County Extension Homemakers Club, the Busy Bees, this week.

On Christmas Day, Kathy's parents, Lillian and Robert Joseph, will be visiting from Great Falls. "My mom will help me cook Christmas dinner," Kathy said.

She plans to keep on directing the junior choir of the First Lutheran Church.

And she's looking forward to this spring, when she'll be able to ride her bicycle.

The pastors and teachers of the Missouri Synod, Montana District, have given her and Bill a tandem bike, a bicycle built for two.

We did spend Christmas Day with them and I did help prepare dinner, but Kathy's gift to Bob was the big news. She'd often heard him say how much fun it would be to have one; but, no, he didn't need one. "Besides, they are very expensive. It's a silly thing to think about—but, it would be fun." What a shock when he opened his gift and there it was—a metal detector.

When Kathy and Bill came to Great Falls for New Years, Bob was ready. He and Bill went out with the metal detector to check the yard. The afternoon passed quickly, and they got out flashlights as it began to get dark. They didn't find buried treasure, but they had a great time!

My mother had been admitted to the hospital between Christmas and New Year. The diagnosis, a lung tumor. She was too weak to have surgery right away, but was kept in the hospital to build up her strength. Surgery on January 13th went well; however, the tumor was cancerous. Her heart problem added to our concern.

Family members took turns staying with Mom to help her and to keep everyone informed of her condition. When Mom went home from the hospital at the end of January, I stayed with her for ten days. My sister came to stay with her then, and I planned to take the bus back to Great Falls. Bill and Kathy called and Kathy said they had wanted to help too, so they had bought a plane ticket for me. I was to pick it up at the airport and my trip home would take thirty minutes instead of six hours. I protested—it was too much money. They reminded me of how much I enjoy helping people; I had no right to deny them the same pleasure. It was good to have such a fast trip home!

By March, Mom was living at St. John's Lutheran Home. Bill and Kathy had gone to visit her often. Her condition continued to deteriorate, we all had been to see her the previous weekend. My sister-in-law called a few days later to say that Mother was worse. I called Kathy and Bill and they drove to Billings and had devotions with Mom. She told me on the phone that evening how thankful she was that they had come. Their devotions were very comforting. That night she died. A memorial service was held at Trinity Lutheran Church in Billings; she was buried in Plevna.

Mom had told Bill at one time, "You should get a color TV."

Bill had chuckled. Kathy couldn't see it anyway. They would rather have a stereo which they could both enjoy.

Mom would have been happy to know that when her belongings were given away, Bill and Kathy received her color TV.

In the spring, The Rev. Fred Naumann interviewed Kathy and Bill for Lutheran Tape Ministry. Rev. Naumann had been Kathy's professor at Concordia Teachers College when she had traveled with the Ambassadors for Christ. The following article appeared in the LWML *Quarterly*.

Mr. and Mrs. Bill Zastrow of Bozeman have helped create a tape for Lutheran Tape Ministry, which has just been released, and already scores of tapes are in circulation. Bill and kathy share ideas on how they, their faith, and their friends help them cope with terminal illness. They have lived with the knowledge of Kathy's cancer for five years. "I am warmed by their faith and am thankful to share their witness," said LTM producer Rev. Fred Naumann. He continued, "Anyone who has or can help the terminally ill ought to be encouraged by these cassette tapes." As one pastor-counselor listener wrote: "Thank you for helping us be informed about coping with terminal illness and how to counsel people suffering from its effects...We have nothing like it in our known resources." In the two tapes, a medical doctor is also interviewed and shares with the listener information about the stages of terminal illness, coping, and advice to others on how they can help. Write , 124 So. 124th St., Omaha, NE 68102. There is no charge for the tape. Donations are appreciated.

The tapes #164 and #165 have been comforting to me. The joy of Kathy's voice lifts my spirits and I've learned by listening to both Kathy's and Bill's tapes. There are many points you just don't think of until you find yourself in a situation like theirs, or unless you've experienced the death of a spouse or child. We can all learn from someone who's been there.

Bill and Kathy made a trip to San Francisco for Kathy's checkup that spring. We were told she'd received a good report. She didn't look good to us. We were afraid that they would not want us to worry and would tell us the report was good no matter what the doctor had said. I worried more than ever.

In June Kathy and Bill informed us that Bill had submitted his resignation to First Lutheran. They would be moving to St. Louis where Bill would attend Concordia Seminary to become an ordained minister.

Under ordinary circumstances I would have been thrilled. But St. Louis was so far away, and so large—how would Kathy cope with all that change? After much prayer, I received peace from God, being reassured that He is in control and He would be with Kathy.

The LWML Convention was in Milwaukee that June and I was gone over Father's Day. Bill and Kathy spent a few days with Bob. He came home one noon and found the note from Kathy included on the next page. He enjoyed their visit.

They went on from Great Falls to Glasgow and spent the rest of their vacation in Smelser's cabin on Ft. Peck Lake. Bill was proud of a 37 1/2 " northern pike he'd caught and Kathy was happy for him.

That summer Bob's sister Roberta and her husband Delbert came to visit. They went on to Bozeman to visit with Bill and Kathy too. Jerl, Debbie and Amos went to Kathy and Bill's first, then they all came to Great Falls to visit. Kathy was not feeling well when they arrived. Bill called a Great Falls doctor, who called doctors in Bozeman and Billings, then called in a prescription for Kathy.

She continued to be more upset than usual. She wanted her hair cut, so I did it for her. While I was giving her the haircut, she broke down in tears. "Mom," she cried, "I know I'm not going to live very long," But her concern was not for herself. "Be sure you are good to Bill." The words haunted me. Why would she worry about how we would treat Bill?

We called several times that weekend after they returned to Bozeman to check on Kathy, but it was Labor Day Weekend, and the doctor was out of town. Early Tuesday morning Bill called to say Kathy was in the hospital in Bozeman. She had shingles and was

Thy word is a lamp unto my feet, and
a light unto my path. Ps. 119:105

Dad,

Bill asked me to eat with him. I will see you later and have supper with you. Hope your day is

going well Kathy

A NOTE FROM KATHY — FATHERS
DAY WEEKEND 1981.
BEAUTIFUL VERSE!

very sick. I can still hear Bill's words. "Mom, if you've ever prayed for Kathy, pray for her now. This is serious." We continued to pray.

Once again Kathy rallied. She was released from the hospital ten days later. I saw Kathy that weekend. The shingles had settled in her eyes, the weakest point in her body. Sometimes they itched so badly, she would rub her eyes until they were raw. At that time, Kathy began to gain weight; she had no control of her appetite.

Kathy looked a little better when we spent Thanksgiving with them. We were all thankful for the improvement.

Bill and Kathy wanted to spend that Christmas with Bill's family. They had enough money for one ticket to Minnesota, so we bought the other for them. Bob and I went to Baker to spend the holiday with my family. We all missed Mom, but we were happy for her—just imagine, Christmas in heaven with Jesus!

IX

It was a Sunday evening, the middle of January, when Bill called. He'd been to Ennis to preach, as usual, but Kathy had stayed home alone. He had returned to Bozeman and found her in the basement hallucinating. She was wet, cold and carrying on a conversation with my mother.

We were very concerned and went to see her the following weekend. At times she was fine; at times she was off in a world of her own.

The Rev. Huber, President of the Montana District of the Lutheran Church-Missouri Synod, and his wife had gone to see Kathy and Bill. Kathy was out in the kitchen when someone in the living room commented, "You just can't be sure of anything these days." Though Kathy had lost her senses of sight, taste and smell, there was nothing wrong with her hearing. She came into the room to respond to the comment.

"Oh yes you can. You can be sure of heaven if you believe in Jesus Christ for your salvation."

It was hard to leave Kathy at the end of the weekend. We worried about her being alone, but we knew Bill would be next door at the church and would go home often to check on her. We also knew she had many friends who would help Bill keep an eye on her. I phoned often, just to check on her and to visit with her.

In February, Bill had a meeting in Missoula, during which Kathy came and stayed with us. She went to Bible Class with me and went along to visit the nursing homes and shut-ins with me. On Valentine's Day she received the gift that had become her traditional gift from Bill—tulips. She could no longer see or smell them, but she could feel them and remember. She missed Bill, but he called often. I'm thankful we had that time together. We spent our evenings just sitting and talking. We shared some beautiful memories.

In March the Good Shepherd Auxiliary had a meeting in California. As President of the Montana Unit, I was expected to attend. Bob had some vacation time left, and I wanted him to go along. He called Kathy to check on her. She said, "I'm fine. Yes, you go, but bring me some Reagan jelly beans and oranges from California."

We called several times while we were there. They called out to wish Bob a happy birthday on March 17. When we called on the 20th, Kathy told us that she and Bill were being interviewed by Robin Mueller for an article for *The Lutheran Witness*, one of our church's publications. Kathy laughed, "Just think, now I'm going to be famous and I won't even be able to read it."

The next day she told Bob the interview had gone well, but she had slept a lot. "You know sleep helps me feel better after a big day."

The interview appeared in the June magazine.

While majoring in history at Mankato State University, Bill Zastrow was living at home in Good Thunder, Minnesota in 1973. Because his love of music included the trombone, piano and singing, it was no surprise that he joined his church choir at St. Johns.

The surprise was Kathy Joseph, a recent graduate of Concordia Teachers College in Seward, Nebraska, and a Montana native. She taught third through fifth graders at St. Johns' and also directed the choir.

"I couldn't get her out of my mind," says Bill, "Kathy communicated with smiles, warm hugs, and encompassed everyone in the congregation. Her smile just said 'Jesus Christ.' You could see it in her playing with kids, visiting homes—living it was her ministry."

The following May they began dating..."We had music in common at first, but we could talk so easily, share so openly—about anything," she explains in her bright sweet voice.

Bill quickly gets to the heart of her effect on him. "She changed me from a pew-warmer to a believer. She witnessed to me, brought me around to a deeper faith in Christ."

Their year of dating often prevented Kathy from thinking about how hazy and out-of-focus things sometimes seemed. Her doctors diagnosed the symptoms as migraine headaches.

After telling about their wedding, the findings of the eye examination and the first surgery, the article continues with:

From Oct. 6 to Nov. 25, she received maximum dosages of radiation and cobalt treatments at the Mayo Clinic. "Kathy, when I'd see you on the weekends, it was just like dating again," Bill remembers. They attended University of Minnesota football games on the weekends and hosted a Halloween party for fifty children in their home...

"I can't ever remember being angry at God," says Kathy. "I just told myself the whole time, 'There's good coming out of this. I know God won't forget me or ever leave me alone.'"

"The anger came later," says Bill. "We thought the worst was behind us."....

And so in June 1980, Kathy became the 32nd person in the world to have radium seeds of Iodine 135 isotope planted in her brain. She was awake during the entire surgery at the University of San Francisco. Three days after surgery she left the hospital.

"By 1:30 that afternoon, we had ridden the streetcars, walked along the wharf, and gone to Oakland for a ballgame," she laughs....

When she returned to Deaconess Hospital in Billings in February 1981, the medical team listened in awe to their stories of outdoor picnics, movies (Bill "filled in" the visual for Kathy), normal home life, and continuing ministry—all for a woman whose death they had predicted a year ago....

"Living with cancer reaches beyond the four corners of the church," says Bill. Make Today Count—a nationwide group of terminal cancer patients—works to encourage each other, and Kathy became a local member. Both Bill and Kathy saw

counselors, medical teams, and social workers to help them cope with the anger and frustration they sometimes experienced.

"I'm not immune—I sometimes am ready to break my cane and hang it up," admits Kathy. "I get the 'poor me's.'"

The woman who now sits in First's parsonage telling her story so matter-of-factly bears little resemblance to the petite, energetic, and somewhat naive young bride in her wedding pictures. But her spirit hasn't changed.

"Her personality and her mind say, 'Go!' but her body just can't do it anymore," Bill whispers. "

"My peers now are old men who have lost their wives to cancer," says Bill. "But they saw their children and grandchildren. I feel cheated; I feel like we've been short-changed."

"Do you really?" Kathy answers. "I don't. We had more in our seven years together than many people have in a lifetime. And I still say God can do anything—anything. We still don't know what He has in store for us." ....

"It is hard to think about death sometimes," Kathy says, and her voice cracks a bit. "But I know I'll have no more blindness, no more pain, no more problems. It will be such a joy! The worst part about dying is leaving Bill—I worry about him being alone."

"I won't be alone," he says softly.

"I'm only 28 years old and I feel like such an old man," sighs Bill. "So much has already happened to me. I've grieved for Kathy's loss of sight. I've grieved for her loss of sexuality. I've grieved for her fears. I've grieved for the loss of my buddy."

"You mean I'm not your buddy anymore?" she half-teases, half-worries.

"Kathy, Kathy," he shakes his head, "We can't hike, we can't play golf, we can't play tennis anymore. You're—"

"Well, I'd say we weren't the greatest tennis players to start with—" They both giggle, remembering sunny afternoons....

"This isn't a great healing testimonial, a typical success story," Bill says slowly, tears filling his eyes. "Our success story

is in the Resurrection. We're all terminal. We're all going to die.
We all have the free gift of eternal life in Jesus Christ."

Kathy agrees by nodding; because her smile is always constant.

Our meeting ended on Monday. Bob already had the jelly beans; a friend took us to get the oranges. We had dinner out and returned to the motel saying good-bye to our friends. We would be flying back to Montana in the morning.

As we entered the room, we noticed the message light was on. We called the office. Bill was trying to reach us. We called their home—no answer.

The phone rang; it was Bill. Kathy had collapsed at the dinner table and he had rushed her to the hospital. They had given her a shot, she was still able to talk, but we should hurry home.

The flight we were scheduled to take was the next one leaving. We would have to wait!

We left Orange County airport at 9:30 the next morning, transferred planes in Salt Lake City and arrived in Great Falls in a snow storm. Our pastor's daughter, Dawn, was at the airport to give us a ride home.

Bob drove to the bank and got the car ready for the drive to Bozeman. I quickly packed clean clothes and in less than an hour we were on our way to Bozeman.

It was snowing harder. We hoped we would get through the mountains before dark. After Helena the snow was worse. We crept along, praying that Kathy would still be alive when we got there.

We finally reached Bozeman at 8:30 and went directly to the hospital. Kathy was aware of our entrance, but unable to speak, she made a noise to greet us.

We talked with Bill. The hospital had given him permission to stay in Kathy's room. Around 10:00 we went to Bill and Kathy's home. We stopped on the way and bought groceries for breakfast. We knew Bill's folks were coming, so we changed bedding for them. We cleaned house until finally we thought we were tired enough to sleep.

We were up early the next morning, had a quick breakfast and hurried to the hospital. We spent the morning praying with Kathy, assuring her of our love.

Bill did not want to leave Kathy, but he was scheduled to teach his youth class a lesson on death and dying. It was too important a class to cancel. He had them come to Kathy's room where he conducted a class I'm sure those students will never forget.

Members of the church brought meals to Bill so he could stay with Kathy.

I went to the parsonage to write my report on the California meeting. The phone rang. It was Wayne, one of the young people who'd made the love banner for Kathy.

"Mrs. Jophes, is Kathy bad sick?"

"Yes, she is."

"Is she going to die?"

"Yes." I began to cry.

"Don't cry, Mrs. Jophes. Kathy will be with Jesus. She loves Him. He will take her to heaven."

"Yes, Wayne."

"I pray for Kathy." He hung up.

I thanked God for the retarded man who could comfort me. I prayed that others would hear his love for God and believe that truth.

The following morning Pastor Lutz came and had devotions in Kathy's room. She still could not speak; however, when Pastor said, "Let's pray Luther's Morning Prayer," she quickly folded her hands.

Throughout the day Bob sang hymns and read Psalms to Kathy. Whenever he would stop she would become restless. Bill would choose the songs and the Psalms, he knew her favorites; Bob would sing and read.

Bill's folks arrived and I went home to give them a chance to visit. Bob came a little later and said, "Oh How I wish I knew what Kathy was trying to tell me when I said goodnight. She just rattled on and on."

Something awakened me suddenly in the morning. I touched Bob. "Hurry. We need to get to the hospital." We showered quickly and left. We arrived at 7:00 to find Kathy breathing very rapidly. Bill said she had been like that nearly an hour. We called Pastor Lutz.

101

After Pastor's prayer, Kathy's breathing slowed down. We were all at her side at 8:25 when we could feel her life drain from her body. It was as though Jesus took her by the hand and led her peacefully to heaven. Her pain had ended.

It was exactly two years after that day when the doctor had answered my question with, "Eighteen months to two years."

X

We had purchased a cemetery plot in Billings when Kathy was just two years old. We mentioned it to Bill; he agreed it would be best to have Kathy buried there.

Bill had expressed his wish to use the funeral pall and we requested people send memorials instead of flowers.

In the morning, Bob and I went to the florist and bought a single rose to pin inside the casket. We then went to the mortuary and I fixed Kathy's hair.

People from church began bringing food and our relatives started arriving. By Sunday evening, our brothers and sisters were all there. People in Bozeman offered rooms for everyone to stay. Bob went with each one to be certain they'd found the home they were staying in and had gotten settled. I made one last trip to the funeral home, alone, and cried.

Monday, the day of the funeral, was a typical spring day. Snow falling one moment; sun shining the next. People came from all over; family, friends, McKesson employees, church workers and students.

Kathy wanted her funeral to be a celebration of praise and thanksgiving. She had been faithful unto death and had claimed her crown of life. She had chosen hymns of joy: "Lift High the Cross," "The Strife is O'er," "The Lord's My Shepherd," "For All the Saints," "I Know That My Redeemer Lives!" The Children's Choir sang "Children of the Heavenly Father," and Darcy Holland sang "Jesus Christ the Apple Tree." The sermon, "I am the Resurrection and the Life," was based on John 11:25-27.

After the service a dinner was served in the church basement. It was important to have time to talk with family and friends, to remember Kathy with them.

We drove to Billings for the burial, where still more friends and relatives had gathered. We had time to visit with them at Trinity Lutheran Church where a lunch was served after the committal service. We said goodbye to our relatives and, with our niece Ruth, returned to Bozeman.

Bob got up early the next morning and took Ruth to the airport. I gathered our belongings and we returned to Great Falls. It took hours to read the mail that had come. Letters of consolation were very meaningful.

Twelve days later, a final tribute to Kathy by Joan Haines appeared in the *Chronicle*.

Kathy: Tribute to a Liver

Since today is Easter, I'd like to write about a woman whose life was synonymous with faith.

The woman is Kathy Zastrow, who lived in Bozeman for the past five years. Kathy died March 26 from a brain tumor.

About seven years ago, one month after Kathy and Bill Zastrow were married, they learned that Kathy had a tumor.

Two years ago, most of the brain tumor was removed. Kathy's optic nerve was also taken out because it was entwined around the growth. The entire tumor couldn't be removed because it was located to close to the brain.

The tumor was found to be malignant. In another operation, radium seeds were implanted near the core of the growth. In the succeeding years, the tumor decreased markedly in size.

Because her optical nerve was removed, Kathy was blind. Blind but undaunted. She learned to walk the streets with a cane and to prepare meals. She studied braille. She insisted on doing chores about the house herself.

Bill is youth education director of the First Lutheran Church. Kathy continued to direct the junior choir at the church. She and Bill also sang with the Bozeman Symphony Chorus.

Kathy attended meetings of Make Today Count, a group for people concerned with serious illness. She made many visits to people stricken with cancer to help them accept their condition and struggle to live as fully as possible.

Kathy was a liver. She was so grateful to be alive. She was so enthusiastic about people. She always had a hug and kind words for her friends. Her friends were many.

About two months ago, her condition changed markedly. She began sleeping for longer and longer periods of time.

Bill said she knew she was dying. One day they sat down together and wrote her funeral service. Kathy picked out the readings and songs. She chose no sad ones.

"Kathy's victory was in giving life to those around her," her husband said.

About 300 people came to her funeral. One little boy came up to Bill afterwards and said, "That's all right, Mr. Zastrow. Kathy's unblinded."

Kathy had a presence, an aura of strength, which remains with the people who knew her. I don't remember Kathy because she was blind or because she had cancer.

I just remember Kathy.

EPILOGUE

We thank God that we had the church, family and friends in those next days. We are especially thankful for Duane and Pam; he was the vicar at our church at that time. Mail continued to arrive. Many memorials were received to be donated to First Lutheran's Pipe Organ Fund, Concordia Teachers College, Lutheran Braille Workers, Good Shepherd Home of the West, Bethesda Home, Trinity Lutheran Parochial School (Billings, MT), and Lutheran Tape Ministry.

The first year after Kathy's death was very hard for us. We suffered a loneliness that you can understand only if you've experienced it. We treasure those friends who would talk about Kathy with us. It hurt when people would avoid mentioning her, as though she had never existed. It still hurts.

There were so many little things that would suddenly, unexpectedly bring Kathy to my mind. We continually found comfort in God's Word.

Finally, on January 21, we read the following devotion:

A mother tells how one evening, when she was tucking her small daughter in bed, the child exclaimed, "Mother, stay with me while I go to sleep." Remembering all the tasks that still awaited her, she hesitated. But seeing the troubled look on the little face, she sat down by the bedside. As the child drifted away to dreamland, the mother bowed her head and prayed, "Lord, when life's evening shall come and I am falling asleep, grant that by grace I too may be able to say, 'Father, take my hand, guide me safely, and receive me when I awaken in glory.'"

Someone has said, "God conceals from us the full happiness that follows death, so that we may be able to endure life." Today you may be sorrowing for a loved one who died trusting in the merits of the crucified and risen Lord Jesus, but actually it is for yourself that you weep. Your dear one is so happy in the mansions above that it is almost sacrilegious for you to selfishly wish him or her back to this dismal land.

Weep not because I walk no longer with you,
Remember I am walking streets of gold;
Weep for yourselves that you awhile must tarry,
Before the blessed Lord you may behold.

————*B.C. Ryberg*

As I read those devotions I felt a release; the burden was being lifted.

On Valentines Day, Bill sent me tulips. They brought back memories of that first delivery, when Bill and Kathy were dating. I could never thank him enough for the love and joy he brought to her life.

In June we went to the LWML Convention in Detroit. We saw Pam and Duane again, visited St. Peter's where Kathy had been a student teacher and were surprised at how many people remembered her and the love they had for her.

Gradually we realized we were adjusting. We will always miss Kathy; but now we can feel happiness for her victory, joy for her peace in Jesus.

We all sin and come short of the Glory of God, as Kathy so often confessed. She gained strength in her time of trials from God's word and would say, "Job did not curse God and neither will I." That courage in witnessing has emboldened me, the depth of her faith has bolstered mine, as it has many who came to know her. Kathy was a sinner, as we all are, her faith was tested, as ours is. My prayer is that in reading this book your faith will be strengthened by Kathy's. Now I, too, find it natural to recognize God's presence control in every part of my life. Now I, too, can speak as easily of Jesus as my best friend, and proclaim his message. "And we know that all things work together for good to them that love God...If God is for us, who can be against us" Romans 8:28-31.

Bob has retired and we have moved to Billings. Now we have even more time to dedicate to volunteer church work.

Bill did go to the Seminary. He has remarried and has served his vicarage. We pray that God will bless him abundantly and that he will be a blessing to the Kingdom of God.

God truly does provide!

Order Form

Forward books ordered below to:

Name: _____

Address: _____

City/State/Zip: _____

Proceeds from book sales are being donated to the charities that touched Kathryn's life, in memory of her, throughout the U.S.A.

_____ copies at $5.00 plus $1.50 postage
and handling   Total: $ _____

Make checks payable to: God's Gift Memorial

Orders above, and inquiries from any Lutheran organization desiring to order and resell large quantities of this book to further the work of a group or as a scholarship fund raising project to one of our Lutheran colleges, in memory of Kathryn, should be directed to:

God's Gift Memorial

Jesus is Our Lord & Savior
Mr. & Mrs. Robert Joseph
3254 Granger Ave. East D6
Billings, MT 59102-6048